ONLY GOD CAN MAKE A BUZZARD

ONLY GOD CAN MAKE A BUZZARD

ROBERT M. BLAZAK

CITI OF BOOKS

CITIOFBOOKS, INC.
3736 Eubank NE Suite A1
Albuquerque, NM 87111-3579
www.citiofbooks.com

Hotline: 1 (877) 389-2759
Fax: 1 (505) 930-7244

Ordering Information:
Quantity sales. Special discounts are available on quantity purchases by corporations, associations, and others. For details, contact the publisher at the address above.

Printed in the United States of America.

ISBN-13:	Softcover	978-1-959682-65-3
	Hardcover	978-1-960952-71-4
	eBook	978-1-959682-66-0

Library of Congress Control Number: 2023900233

A wonderful example of how to raise a family on a shoestring budget with love, faith and determination. Living in the country, away from the noise and mayhem of city life, children can grow to love nature and not rely on friends, computers and babysitters to entertain them.

This book candidly teaches the reader how to create a firm foundation for their children.

In the late 1940s, Cam and Emil Blazak and their three young children lived in Parma, Ohio, a suburb of Cleveland. They wanted their kids to live in a more stress-free environment where they could learn and experience nature. They found a small farm in Hinckley, Ohio, about 25 miles south of the big city. Hinckley is known for its "National Buzzard Day" and "Buzzard's Roost," which is adjacent to our farm. Thus the title, Only God Can Make a Buzzard. This began an adventure that truly created the foundation for my future.

I was seven when we moved to my "enchanted kingdom," and these stories are experiences that I recall from my early years on the farm. You'll notice that, in almost every story. my parents were there to guide and watch over me as I stumbled my way toward adulthood. The stories will take you from belly laughs to tears and back.

You'll also find that God is the center of our family as I relate each story to a Bible verse to show you that everything that happens in life, good and bad, is addressed and answered in God's word, if you just take the time to read it.

CONTENTS

Dedication i

PREFACE. iii

SPRINGTIME. 1

SNAKE IN THE GRASS 2

THE GREAT DOG HUNT. 5

THE WEEMA HOMESTEAD 7

LIGHTNING AND THE SHOE TREES 11

THE RUNAWAY BROTHER 14

MAY FLOWERS AND SHOTGUNS 17

GERONIMO 22

SUMMERTIME 27

TIN HELICOPTERS 28

FORTS AND LOOKOUTS. 31

SLINGSHOTS AND DAIRY FARMS. 35

DAM DIVING. 38

LOSING A FRIEND 43

THE DRUM MAJOR 48

THE LEGENDARY LEDGES. 51

SOUNDS OF A SUMMER'S NIGHT 55
THE ARMCHAIR SCOUTMASTER.......57
CYCLING 61
THE FALL............................65
GREEN APPLES AND APPENDICITIS....66
PAINTING THE ROOF 69
GARDEN FRESH 72
HAY! DON'T SMOKE!!!................76
WINTER WONDERLAND 78
IGLOOS IN OHIO? 79
SLEDS VS. ANTHILLS.................84
BOW HUNTING RABBITS..............87
BUZZARD HUNTING..................90
THE FIRST KISS 93
THE "WALLED-OFF ASSTORIA" 97
BUZZARDS AGAIN 101
PARTY ON WHEELS 104
EYE FOR AN EYE.....................107
CHRISTMAS.........................110
FOOTBALL SEASON...................112
EPILOGUE 115
WHERE ARE THEY NOW?.............117
THE PERFECT LOVE STORY...........119

Dedication

To Mom and Dad, Mr. and Mrs. B, Cam, and Emil. Without their love and guidance, this book would never be. Thanks, of course, to God for His love and guidance in each and every one of our lives.

Our childhood is the foundation of our lives.

PREFACE

We all have good times and bad times in our lives. I was blessed with having an eight-year period in my life that was so wonderful and exciting that it formed my personality and direction in life. I was also blessed with the most wonderful, loving parents anyone could ever dream of.

When I was 7 years old, my parents, my brother Dick, my sister Sue, and I were living in Parma, Ohio, a suburb of Cleveland. My dad worked for Western Union Telegraph Company and he and my mom decided to raise our family in the country, away from the hectic city life. Mom and Dad found a special place in Hinckley, Ohio, about 25 miles south of Cleveland. This was to become our new home and we moved there in the summer of 1949.

They bought a 100-year-old farm on fifty acres that were surrounded on three sides by the Cleveland Metropolitan Park System. There was a chicken farm across the road and nothing more for what seemed like miles. The house had electricity and a coal furnace but was without water. Once a working farm, it was in disrepair with several out buildings including a big barn and sheds.

The stories that follow are some of my memories of those wonderful years as I recall them. Many friends and relatives have graciously helped me relate some of these experiences to the bible and hymns popular in our church, Roswell Presbyterian Church, in Roswell, Georgia, where I currently live. I was baptized, raised, and nurtured at Parma South Presbyterian Church in Parma, Ohio. I'm 81 now, and the adventures I had as a child seem as though they just occurred yesterday. They might not be stone-cold accurate, but pretty close. I think it's interesting to note how clear our memories are of our childhood, yet we can't remember what we did yesterday. Time can reasonably distort recollection. There may be an occasional embellishment and a dash of poetic license occur but it's only to add flavor to a rare mundane moment.

I might add that reconstruction often breeds some form of fantasy. Times and dates will blend over the years, but the essence of the adventures loom bright. I've altered some of the names out of respect and some due to the eroding of my mind over time.

The foundation of my childhood was a set of parents that only God could have matched at His finest moment. They came together from two diverse worlds and backgrounds. Their love and respect for each other permeated my life daily, as did their love of God. They were married for 67 years and anger was as rare as rain on a desert. As a child, growing up in this enchanted kingdom, I never witnessed nor experienced hate.

Somewhere, sometime, there must have been a downside, but I sure as heck can't remember what it was.

There are two themes to this book that are important to note: one, of course, is God's words to Moses in Exodus 20:12, "Honour thy father and thy mother: that thy days may be long upon the land which the Lord thy God giveth thee." The second theme is to show the reader that everything we experience in life, good and bad, is addressed in the Bible. God has answers for all our concerns and offers guidance for every situation in our lives if we will just take the time to search His word. If you will take the time from your busy lives to read the Bible, it will change, improve, and enhance your life forever.

"GOD, YOU DID GOOD!!! THANK YOU"

This is the house after we remodelled the kitchen and utility room on the left side of the main house. About 1951. That's Rags in front of one of the three big maple trees in the front yard.

SPRINGTIME

SNAKE IN THE GRASS

Springtime in Hinckley is a wonderful time of year. However, it can be unpredictable when it comes to weather. We had snow as late as May and temperatures in the 80s a week later. In general, however, spring is a beautiful season with flowers blooming and trees budding everywhere. I loved to walk through the hills, valleys, and woods of our property. Since we were surrounded on three sides by the Metropolitan Park System, I had hundreds of acres in which to wander.

One of my favorite places was a valley about a half mile from the house. To get there I walked along a fire path between two fields. The path was draped with Elderberry bushes that created a tunnel and smelled wonderful. The path then meandered down a hillside to a beautiful green meadow with a babbling stream flowing aimlessly through it. The spring grass was about knee deep and there was an old wooden bridge made of barn planking across it. This was a perfect place to race boats. The water cascaded over rocks and changed directions every few yards. That water was so clean and cold that you could drink it, which I usually did. A boat was simple. It was a piece of stick about four inches long. That's it! Two boats, two sticks, and you needed a longer stick to unstick the stick boats when they got stuck.

On one of those beautiful, sunny, Saturday afternoons, I decided to wander down to the creek and race some boats. I couldn't go blackberry picking and eating yet, because it was too early in the year. Eventually, I arrived at my favorite spot just upstream from the bridge. I had already made my boats on the way there. I carefully tossed them in, making sure they were not touching each other and that one was not ahead of the other. As they started drifting downstream I realized I didn't have a long stick to free them if they got caught on a rock. I looked around the grass near me and saw a black tree branch among the weeds. I reached down and picked it up, planning to break it to the right length for a guide stick.

That was the first time I think my heart ever stopped beating. For a moment, the whole world came to a dead stop. I had just picked up a three-foot black snake. At that time in my life, the only things I feared were spiders and SNAKES. The next thing I recall, I was on the back porch, trying to get my breath and explain to my mom what had happened. Mom said she saw me coming and I might have set a world record for the half mile. When she finally translated my babbling, she quietly explained to me that black snakes were harmless and a big help to farmers because they killed mice and rats. Tell it to the judge! I still hate snakes and always will. To this day, I still enjoy racing sticks down the babbling stream,, but I bring my own boats and stick.

I've tried to remember some stories I learned as a child that related to snakes and could only remember two. One was about some Saint that lead all the snakes out of Ireland and the other was just a misunderstanding. It was about what I thought was from the Bible called "The Serpent on the Mound". My mom often read to us from the Bible and my mind was often elsewhere. It took me years to realize that she was referring to "The Sermon on the Mount".

EXODUS 4:2-3 "And the LORD said unto him, What is that in your hand? And he said, A rod. And he said, Cast it on the ground. And he cast it on the ground, and it became a serpent; and Moses fled from before it."

THE GREAT DOG HUNT

One of the sad and unusual things that happen in the springtime, in the countryside around large cities, has to do with dogs. During the holidays parents get the idea that it would be fun to have a dog. What a wonderful gift for surprising kids. Many are bought just to appease their demanding children with the idea that the dog would make a great substitute for the parent and give the child something to love while they work. This new "toy" lasts about two to three months and the uniqueness wears off. Cost and maintenance override the cuteness and the dog becomes a liability. Instead of giving the poor soul to an animal humane society, these thoughtless people will take the poor dogs out to the country and "dump" them, to survive as best they can.

This was the case in the spring of 1950. We lived about 25 miles south of Cleveland and seeing wild dogs in the spring was all too common. This particular spring was one of the worst. It seemed like every time we went somewhere, we saw a stray or two.

It was on a Sunday afternoon that this problem came to a peak. My dad, mom, brother, and I were in the house changing our clothes after our return from church. Sue, 5 at the time, was playing in the backyard. Suddenly we heard her scream. I can still remember that sound. As we reached the back screen door, we froze in fear and shock. There was my little sister about 30 yards away, surrounded by about 20 dogs, all sizes and shapes, all breeds, some actually frothing at the mouth in their starved and rabid condition.

My dad was the first to react. He told my mom to run and get two 12 gauge shotguns and a box of shells. Then he dashed out with a walking stick that was near the door. Yelling and swinging the stick, he tried to scare off the dogs, but they kept closing in, snarling and nipping at each other and baring their teeth at my dad. My mom loaded both guns and rushed them out to my dad. She had filled her apron pockets with shells and handed my dad the rest.

Thus began the war. After the first three or four biggest dogs were killed, my sister ran to the house on Dad's instructions, and the killing continued until they were all dead. Some ran off, but we counted eighteen when it was all over. Shortly thereafter, dad cranked up the tractor and attached the backhoe. He loaded up the carcasses and buried them in a field well away from the house.

I ask you to remember this story the next time you get an inkling to get a dog for yourself or your family. Owning a dog doesn't always work out as planned, and if it doesn't, please take the dog (or cat) to a shelter and, at least, give it a chance to find a new home where it can be loved and cared for.

SIGN ON A CHURCH BULLETIN BOARD: "Who's your best friend?? DOG or GOD (dog spelled backwards)

THE WEEMA HOMESTEAD

Living in the country involves some unique experiences. One is the fact that you have neighbors that are few and far between. On our farm, we actually had only two neighbors within a mile of us. When my parents bought the farm it was actually forty-nine and one quarter acres. Three-quarters of an acre was owned by our neighbors, The Trefneys. They had a house down the road about a quarter mile away. We rarely saw them and never really got to know them well. Across the road was the Weema Farm. It was on lease from the Cleveland Metropolitan Park System. This system consisted of a series of parks surrounding the Cleveland area and was called the Emerald Necklace. The farm was leased to a family from Holland who made their living primarily by raising chickens and selling eggs and poultry in the city.

When we moved to the farm, Mr. and Mrs. Weema were in their eighties and their son was in his fifties. They were hard workers from the old country and spoke limited English. Garrett, the son was a giant of a man, well over six feet tall and about 250 pounds of solid muscle. He had worked the farm fifteen hours a day for twenty years and seemed like Paul Bunyan to us. His hands were like leather and heavily calloused and scarred from the chickens pecking on them as he took their eggs from under them every day. He had little patience for us "city folk" and after carrying us to the hospital on several occasions, commented that "you darn city folks are going to kill yourselves one of these days."

Garrett gave me my first job on his farm. I was eight and a half and got paid fifty cents an hour. After the eggs were collected, they had to be candled, weighed, and boxed by size for their trip to the city. The candling was done in his dirt cellar where it was dark and damp. The eggs were put in front of a light so that you could see the shadow of the inside of the egg. Sometimes there was a rotten one, sometimes a double yoker, and sometimes you could actually see a baby chick. These were put in special crates, since the double yokers brought extra money. Then the good eggs were weighed and boxed in small, medium, large, and extra large boxes. Three times a week, he would load up his old rickety station wagon and head for the city to cover his route. The eggs packed by the dozen were sold to homes and the crates were sold to stores and restaurants. He also sold chickens, cream, and milk. He had ten cows that were milked every morning, a pasteurizing machine, and a butter chum.

In his spare time, Garrett would prepare, plant, and harvest about seven fields of hay, which he stored in his and our barn. The bails were sold or used to feed his cows in the winter. This was another adventure I'll be telling you about.

One of the many experiences I had at the Weema's was the time I caught a cold working in the cellar. Garrett didn't believe in doctors and fancy medicines, so he took it upon himself to cure me. When lunch time arrived, he ordered me to the kitchen where he created the most ungodly concoction I had ever had. It was composed of two raw eggs, some cream, and a shot of whiskey. I was told to hold my nose and drink it down in one, non-stop gulp. You can bet I created some new faces as it went down. Then he had me lay flat on my back on the hardwood floor for thirty minutes. He had to wake me after 30 minutes, but I never had so much as a sniffle after that. If I felt sick, he would be the last to know.

Over the next six years, I learned a lot about farming from Garrett. He was a great friend and teacher. His parents died a couple of years later and he actually wrote home to Holland and had a wife sent over. When his lease ran out in 1955, he and his wife moved into another farm near Medina. The farm was levelled in recent years and grown over. There is now no sign that it ever physically existed. It will always be there in my mind and heart. Thank you Garrett for those wonderful years.

1 THESSALONIANS 5: 12-13 "And we beseech you, brethren, to know them which labour among you, and are over you in the Lord, and admonish you And to esteem them very highly in love for their work's sake. And be at peace among yourselves."

Psalms 111:3 "His work is honourable and glorious: and his righteousness endureth forever."

This is the Weema house, across the road, taken before they moved in. Today there is no sign the farm ever existed, just dense woods.

LIGHTNING AND THE SHOE TREES

When we first moved into the farmhouse we had three bedrooms. Mom and dad had theirs on the first floor, just off the living room and kitchen. Upstairs were two rooms, one in front and one in the back of the main part of the house. The stairway, which was very narrow and steep, led to my sister's room in the back. We had to walk through her room to get to my brother's and mine. There was an alcove in our room with a slanted ceiling. That was Dick's spot and he had his bed and dresser tucked in nice and cory. There was a big window at the foot of his bed, facing the front of the house. Across the room was my bed. We each had matching twin beds made of cherry that was bought for us when I was born in Parma. I still have most of the set today. In fact, my grandson slept on it when he was little. I got the chest of drawers and it had a neat little center drawer that I used for my special keepsakes.

The window had two panes of glass and could be propped open to let in the night air. Screens were still a distant idea. We would leave the window open in summer and winter since there was no heat upstairs anyway. We had these great feather ticks that were filled with down. My favorite spot in winter was to tack it in on the wall side and slide down off the bed and use it like a hammock between the bed and wall. There were mornings when we would wake up with snow on our beds from the opened window. All The good old days!

Spring brought on the April showers and with the showers, thunder and lightning. About 10:00 one night the wind and rain were kicking up pretty well. It was usually warm, which probably added to the storm. We had a tin roof then and the rain on the roof was like a tranquilizer. The window, as usual, was open since the wind and rain were pelting the back of the house. The maple tree outside the window rustled and added to the many sounds of the night. I was just about asleep when Dick spoke up and asked if the water was leaking in. I looked toward the window as distant lightning lit the room.

Suddenly, as if on cue, the entire room seemed to explode. It was as if someone had just stuck a flash camera in my face and snapped it. There was a deafening explosion and I was thrown against the wall next to my bed. Lightning has a way of finding metal and the lightening rod on the roof was missing. Somehow it found the open window and spotted my brother's metal shoe trees at the foot of his bed. When I regained control of my wits and bladder, I turned on my light to see the room filled with smoke. At the foot of Dick's bed, where his shoe trees used to be, was a hole about a foot wide, still smoldering. The foot board on his bed was scorched, but since it was wood and not grounded, Dick was unhurt.

We didn't sleep well for the next couple of weeks and to this day, whenever I hear thunder, I check to make sure the windows are closed and there aren't any metal shoe trees laying around.

PSALM 29:4"The voice of the LORD is powerful; the voice of the LORD is full of majesty."

THE RUNAWAY BROTHER

The first spring after we moved to the farm, I had settled into my new enchanted land. My brother, however, was not quite so content. Since he was a little older, he had made friends in the city and missed them, and living in the country with no neighbors nearby, was a difficult adjustment for him. As spring sprung and the birds sang, and the weather got better, he made the wild decision to "go home and live with his old friends. Since Mom and Dad wouldn't move back to the city, he felt that the only way to accomplish this mission was to run away from his new home in the country.

On one hot Saturday afternoon in May, and after an unsuccessful discussion with Mom, he decided to head for the city on his own. Putting on a well-worn pair of old blue jeans, an old tee shirt, and his favorite Keds; he headed for the door. Mom, with her infinite wisdom and calm demeanor, explained we all loved him and would prefer that he stay, but if he was insistent on leaving, he could go if he wished. There was, however, the one simple rule involved in leaving that he needed to obey," If you choose to leave, you cannot take or wear anything that we bought for you."

To some kids, this would end any idea of leaving, but Dick, however, was determined to find a way to accomplish his task. "Can't" was not to be part of his vocabulary. Ten minutes later he appeared in a pair of old socks that he had gotten for Christmas from an aunt and a two-year-old, faded and torn bathing suit. "These are Jimmy's (a cousin) and you didn't buy them.", he said. Mom said "OK." and he was headed out the door and off to the city to rejoin the friends he had left behind.

I can still remember looking out the window and watching my big brother scooting across the yard and heading for the gravel road that would take him on his journey. Every year, in the spring, the county would come by with a big oil truck and spray the gravel road with tar in front of each house to keep the dust down. If the temperature got over seventy degrees, the tar would get tacky and smell terrible. Walking in socks, on or near the road, was not a good idea for obvious reasons. I watched him dance and tiptoe his way about one hundred yards northbound toward Cleveland until he finally decided that maybe his plan might not be the greatest. Of course, Mom was watching all this from another window, knowing the outcome in advance. He finally jumped the ditch that ran alongside the road and sat down on a grassy bank to revise his plan. He now had to figure out how to return home and still maintain some degree of dignity.

His new plan was TIME! If he sat there long enough, maybe everyone would forget about his idea to run away to the big city. Mom always being one step ahead of us, instructed both Sue and me not to say anything and act as if nothing had happened. After about an hour, Dick slipped into the house and headed straight to his bedroom where he ditched the socks in a wastebasket, carefully hidden under some papers, and redressed in his jeans and favorite Cleveland Brown's logo tee shirt. By now it was dinner time and we were all called to dinner, which was especially good that night as we all tried

15

to avoid talking about the event that had gone awry that afternoon. Looking at each other across the table, Sue and I shared a secret together and just rolled our eyes and grinned knowingly.

Luke 17:3-4   "Take heed to yourselves: If thy brother trespass against thee, rebuke him: and if be repent, forgive him. And if he trespass against thee seven times in a day. and seven times in a day turn again to thee, saying, I repent; thou shalt forgive him."

Samuel 16:7   "But the Lord said unto Samuel, Look not on his countenance, or on the height of his stature; because I have refused him: for the Lord seeth not as man seeth; for man looketh on the outward appearance, but the Lord looketh on the heart."

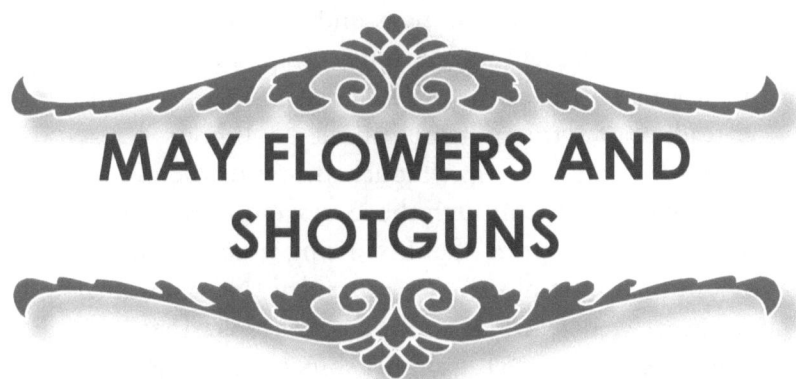

MAY FLOWERS AND SHOTGUNS

Near the back of our property was a tract of land owned by a Mr. Stewart. There is a long history connected to this property that gives a good foundation for this unusual story. Today it is an historic homestead called "The Worden Heritage Homestead". In the early 1950's it was owned by a man named Noble Stewart who spent much of his time carving figures in the ledges behind his home. These ledges, now called "Worden's Ledges", were an enchanting and mysterious place for two young adventurous boys like Dick and I. The problem was that old Mr. Stewart didn't like kids and protected his lodges from intruders like us.

The next piece of the puzzle is a plant called "The May Apple, or Terillium". Very common in the northeast, the May Apple would bloom in the spring with a white flower that hung beneath a large hand-shaped leaf. Later in the year, the flower would develop into a small apple. They flourished in the shaded woods and damp, rich ground of the rolling hills around Hinckley.

On one of those sunny, warm weekends, Dick and I decided to go exploring and the carvings were just a story at that time. We put on our hiking Keds, belt with hunting knife, first aid kit, and compass, and filled our canteens with Kool-Aid. We were Indiana Jones, Captain Midnight, and Will Robinson (from the TV's "Lost in Space"), combined, and ready for anything. It took about a half hour to reach the first signs of the carvings. Crouched low to the ground and tip- toeing carefully through the leaves and timber, we saw, to our amazement, a stone "Sphinx" rising from the underbrush. "This must be the place!", we mumbled. Now on our hands and knees, we crawled closer for a better look. Then we began to see more carvings: A big clipper ship, heads of men we didn't know, a big cross, a wooden bridge with writing all over it, and a small log cabin. There were stone lined walkways everywhere and we were in awe.

Suddenly there was an eery feeling like we were not alone. There were no birds, no sounds, and we could feel eyes watching us. I looked down at my feet and saw something very strange. The May Apples had purple flowers on them. I pointed them out to my brother and he suggested we dig up some and take them home. With one eye searching the area for the unknown, I took out my trusty hunting knife and started to dig up some plants. My heart was pounding like a machine gun and I was sweating profusely, but I kept digging. Suddenly, the silence was broken by the loud, deep, shout of what could have been Bigfoot, Frankenstein, and a Werewolf all in one. It echoed through the trees like a loud speaker at school. "You kids get out of here now or I'll shoot you all dead!"

I couldn't move! I dropped the plants and my prize hunting knife, turned toward the bottom of the hill, and ran like I had never ran before. As I started to sprint off into the woods, I heard a gun shot and pellets hitting the trees above me. This caused me to stumble and fall several times. About

200 yards from the carvings, Dick and I collapsed and lay in the leaves trembling and breathless. Then, as if anticlimactic, we heard the scariest laugh from the hilltop above us. I can still remember it to this day and cringe.

That got us to our feet again and we danced through another 200 yards of underbrush, blackberry bushes, and creek beds. By the time we got home, we were a sight for sore eyes. Torn clothes, mud, scratches and totally exhausted. Dad met us in the yard and asked what happened. Slowly he pulled the story out of us and became furious. Moments later he was in his car heading for the Stewart house to give the old man a piece of his mind.

That's the last time I saw purple May Apples, the carvings, and my hunting knife for almost 20 years. In 1975, my sister, who is now the curator for the Hinckley Historical Society, and I revisited the carvings and I retraced our adventure. Low and behold, stuck in the ground, rusted and rotted, was my trusty hunting knife, right where I had dropped it.

You can visit the carvings today and learn about the history of the area. Just contact the Cleveland Metroparks at 216-635-3264 for information.

Romans 5:15   "But not on the offence, so also is the free gift. For if through the offence of one many be dead, much more the grace of God, and the gift by grace, which is by one man, Jesus Christ, hath abounded unto many."

Psalms 23:4 "Yea, though I walk through the valley of the shadow of death, I will fear no evil."

Psalms 56:4 "In God I will praise his word, in God I have put my trust; I will not fear what flesh can do unto me."

Psalms 27:2 "When the wicked, even mine enemies and my foes, came upon me to eat up my flesh, they stumbled and fell."

Proverbs 14:3   "In the mouth of the foolish is a rod of pride: but the lips of the wise shall preserve them."

Proverbs 13:3   "He that keepeth his mouth keepeth his life: but he that openeth wide his lips shall have destruction."

This is the carving of a sphinx we saw as we approached the area of the carvings.

GERONIMO

I n the late fifties and early sixties, the Scouting Organization added a new dimension to its overall program from Cub Scouts to Boy Scouts to two special groups for boys 14 and up. One was called Sea Scouts and the other was called Explorers. The Explorers wore dark green uniforms with brown man's dress ties and had their own achievement levels reaching to the equivalent of the Boy Scout Eagle rank called The Silver Award. Their activities were geared for teenagers and young adults and their field trips were aimed at preparing the young men for their futures.

In the spring of 1956, I completed my Eagle Award and joined a group of boys that had just started the first Explore Post at our church. My Dad and brother also joined the group and one of our first trips was a weekend at Clinton County Air Force Base near Dayton, Ohio. We were invited along with about 80 other Explores from the Cleveland Area to spend a weekend on the base learning what it was like being in the Air Force.

We spent Friday night in the barracks under the direction of five Sergeants assigned to us. After dinner in the mess hall, we were given our assignments for the balance of the weekend. Following breakfast we were to prepare for jump training.

We would learn how to check out our parachutes, connect to static lines and practice sliding down a long line from a tower to a sand pit. In The morning we were divided into groups of 20 and assigned to two officers who would put us through our paces. One of the instructors was a typical drill Sergeant and thought he was a cross between Audie Murphy, John Wayne, and Sergeant Bilko. He had a need to make us feel like idiots. He would yell orders and threaten to make us do push-ups if we didn't obey every command quickly. I was later requested to keep his name in confidence, so I'll just refer to him as Sergeant Bilko.

After the training and lunch, we were issued parachutes and led to a C130 Flying Boxcar Cargo Plane waiting on the tarmac. The chutes varied in size based on the user's weight. No one paid any attention to who got what size and I ended up with a chute that must have been made for 2400 pound giant. I was pushing 120 pounds at the time. We boarded the plane and sat along the side walls, ten on each side. In the center was a Bombay door that could be opened and used for the jumper's exit. We were instructed to connect our static lines to a cable above our heads. When we jumped, this line would automatically open our chute, but no one was actually going to jump, although it sure seemed real at the time.

My dad and brother were in my group and sitting across from me. We took off and climbed to about 1500 feet, circling the airfield. Then, to our surprise, Sergeant Bilko opened the Bombay doors so we could see the ground.

"Who wants to jump?" He shouted. I thought it was for real and shouted back, "I'll go, Sir!" Thinking this would be a good time to show off his toughness and make a fool out of me, he shouted back, "Get over here and connect your static, boy."

23

I responded immediately and prepared to jump. He got a good grip on my chute and told me to go on THREE. He counted, ONE, TWO,- - - and I jumped, breaking from his grip. It was a sunny, warm day with no wind. I felt the jerk of the static line and my chute opened perfectly, jolting me to a stop in mid-air. Then I began to float very slowly toward the ground.

As I looked down I could see all kinds of activity on the runway below. Fire trucks, ambulances, jeeps, and trucks were coming from all directions to meet me. I felt like a hero and was looking for a band playing military music, but no one was cheering. It took me so long to get to the ground, because of that huge parachute, that my plane had landed and one jeep had my dad and brother in it along with the base commander. As I was about to touch down I prepared myself to throw my legs to one side and roll as I was trained to do, but I was moving so slow that I touched down and pranced across the concrete like a ballerina just before several soldiers grabbed me and made sure I didn't fall. Everyone was rushing up to me and asking me if I was all right. I was so excited I couldn't respond. I was immediately put into a truck and whisked off to a nearby building and ushered to a room where I was confined with the base commander, my dad, Sergeant Bilko, and a couple other officers.

It was explained to me that I was never supposed to jump from that plane. Sergeant Bilko was reprimanded and later demoted for his actions and I was instructed to keep the whole incident quiet. No medal for me and this is the first time I've told anyone about my experience, except for a couple thousand friends and neighbors and anyone else who would listen over the years. Some things are just too special not to share.

Later that year we moved back to the city and the next chapter in my life was about to begin. That might be another book someday. I'm still looking for a chance to jump again, and I will, while I can still walk and talk.

Hebrews 11:1   "Now faith is the substance of things hoped for, the evidence of things not seen. "

Psalms 14:1"The fool hath said in his heart, There is no God. They are corrupt, they have done abominable works, there is none that doeth good."

Proverbs 10:23 "It is a sport to a fool to do mischief: but a man of understanding hath wisdom."

Philippians 4:6   "Be careful for nothing; but in everything by prayer and supplication with thanksgiving let your requests be made known unto God."

This is a picture of the C-130 Hercules which is similar to the plane that I jumped from.

SUMMERTIME

TIN HELICOPTERS

Growing up on our little country farm gave opportunities for many new and exciting adventures. Some were life-changing and some were just fun. Some were frightening and some left scars that still exist today as a reminder of mistakes we made as kids. This story is about one of those crazy things that just happen, without planning or forethought.

We didn't have a lot of money to buy fancy toys in those days, so when we got something from the store, it was a big deal. My parents had taken the three of us to the five-and-dime store in town on Saturday and we each had a dollar to pick out whatever we wanted. I remember my sister picking out some cut-out books with cardboard models and pages of clothes to cut out and put on the models. She also bought a small pair of scissors to work with. My brother picked out a plastic water pistol. I remember it was green, a strange color for a gun.

My choice was a tin helicopter. It had a stick with a spool on it, a piece of string, and a neat propeller that was made of tin and was cut so that you could bend the blades, as per the instructions, to cause it to lift off and fly when it was spun.

I was really excited to try out my prize, and proud that it was neater than my brother's choice because he quickly dumped his gun and wanted to play with my choice. When we got home, on my mom's insistence, we headed for the backyard to try it out. I unwrapped it and glanced over the instructions. I quickly wound the string on the spool, held it at arms length, and gave it a good yank. The blades quickly lifted and took off like lightning across the yard. "Pretty cool!" I thought to myself. We laughed and ran to retrieve it. Adjusting the blades, we sent it on several more flights until we were able to get it to go straight up and hover for almost fifteen seconds.

Now it was time to share, so I gave it to my brother to try. He was bigger and stronger so he was able to send it above the trees. He carefully wound the string, got a good grip and pulled with a loud grunt. The blades lifted about three inches off the stick and shot like a bullet at that level. The only thing that kept it from landing in the next county was my chin.

In a split second, I was on the ground flopping like a fish out of water and screaming bloody murder. Why did God choose me to be the landing sight for all the strange things man could create. Sleds, helicopters, teeth!!! What next? Maybe a truck!!

Dad was home this time and after securing my chin with cold towels, we were off to our friendly local Medina County Emergency Room for stitches.

Everything we do in life is supposed to teach us something about life and will help us grow into better people. This was a tough lesson to figure out. Well I guess sometimes things just happen. No message. No lesson. No reason. Except this. Never trust a cheap tin helicopter to follow the instructions.

From the hymn "Our God, Out Help in Ages Past", from Psalm 90:1-5

"Our God, our help in ages past,

Our hope in years to come,

Be Thou our guard while life shall last,

And our eternal home."

FORTS AND LOOKOUTS

Living out in the country with no neighbors close by to play with during the summers, my brother, my sister, and I had to find ways to entertain ourselves. That was never a problem since we lived on a 50-acre fantasyland farm where there were several old abandoned chicken coups, a corn crib, a machine shed, a milk house, a grainery, and a huge barn.

When we moved to the farm, my grandparents lived in Florida, but Mom and Dad decided to build a cottage for them behind the house so they could be closer to the family. The plan was, to move the grainery about a hundred feet and use it as a bedroom; then build a living room and kitchen on front of that.

Dad ordered a truckload of concrete blocks to use for the foundation and had them stacked in the backyard, until they were ready to start building. Those blocks needed to be used for something right away, so Dick and I decided to do a little building of our own. Working all of one afternoon, we managed to arrange them into a neat fort with windows on the front side so we could be on the lookout for Indians. We stored our toy guns and handmade weapons inside so that when we rushed for cover, should we spot an Indian sneaking up on us, we had our ammo ready.

Sue was 6 years old at the time, and just one of the "guys". She was the perfect example of the picture in the World Book Encyclopedia under the heading, "Tomboy". When we needed a lookout, she was recruited to the post. Indians were sneaky guys in those days and they could be anywhere, so we needed someone in a high spot that had a good view in all directions. What better spot than on the top of the barn! Her mission was to climb to the top of the barn and if she saw an Indian approaching she was to make the sound of a screaming eagle

To this day, I don't know how she did it, but a few minutes later we heard the sound of a screaming eagle, and looking up toward the barn; there was our little sister on the peak of the roof, hanging on for dear life. The barn was about 50 feet from the ground up to the peak and the roof was brown, rusty tin. How she got there was a mystery as there were no ladders anywhere to be seen. The immediate problem was; she couldn't get down!

As soon as Mom heard all the screeching and commotion, she came running out to see what was going on. When she saw Sue on top of the burn, Dick and I knew we were in big trouble. She sent me running across the road to get Mr. Weema to come and help with the rescue. We helped him get the ladders and some long ropes out of the barn. Leaning the ladder up against the side of the burn, he climbed as high as he could, and tossed the rope to Sue, instructing her to tie the rope around her chest. This done, he lowered her down the back side of the barn and into our waiting arms.

Sue thought it was a blast. She never got scared and actually had no idea what all the fuss was about. I thought she was pretty cool, for a girl. When dad got home, we had a long, serious talk and he made us realize what could have happened. After that, Sue had to watch for Indians from the ground.

The family attended Church and Sunday School every Sunday and that Sunday we all thanked God for watching over my little sister that day. We never did see any Indians in Hinckley after that.

Luke: 40 "Be ye therefore ready also: for the Son of man cometh at an hour when ye think not."

Psalms 32:7 "Thou art my hiding place; thou shalt preserve me from trouble; thou shalt compass me about songs of deliverance. Selah."

Sue could climb anything, including barns, at this age. No Indian or Communist would ever dare confront her.

SLINGSHOTS AND DAIRY FARMS

Schoolmates, Patsy and Jim Kamp were about the same age as my brother and me and lived about a mile down the road from our farm. Their dad owned a huge dairy farm where he processed, bottled, and shipped milk to the local dairies daily. The milk was processed in glass quart jugs which were supplied by the local dairies, including Elm Farm Dairy, which was the dairy that delivered our milk. Each bottle was plugged with a round cardboard seal and then covered with another thin cardboard cap. Mr. Kamp had cases of these caps stored for future use, and these caps turned out to be great projectiles for our newly designed slingshots.

My brother, Dick, had to choose a project for his shop class at school and decided that making a slingshot would not only meet the requirements of the project, but could be used after school for recreational purposes. One of the requirements of the class was to use a power tool, so Dad's table saw covered that part of the construction. Making a plan, he sketched out a "y" shaped slingshot with a rounded handle and notches near the fork of the "y" to insert a large rubber band. He even sanded and stained it to give it a professional look. Much to my amazement, he made two of them; you can't have a battle without an opponent.

We started testing them out with gravel from the roadside but quickly got into trouble by destroying everything breakable, so Dad laid down the law. If we were to keep these weapons of mass destruction, we could only shoot projectiles that did not kill or maim anyone or anything, for which the cats and dogs were very thankful. One afternoon, while visiting our friends, the Kamps, we discovered these boxes of bottle caps and quickly realized that they could be folded into missiles that could sting but were not armor-piercing. Mr. Kamp, being such a great guy, saw the potential and agreed to give us a couple hundred caps, if we made him a promise that we wouldn't shoot them at his cows or any other domestic animals in the area.

Walking down that long dirt road, slingshots in hand, and a pocket full of bottle caps, we were ready to shoot at anything and everything, including each other. We didn't see any wild animals, cats, dogs, deer, Communists, or Indians for months. They know we had the ultimate weapons and ruled the world. Although at times we were tempted to try them out on each other.

Ahh, those were the great days of summer. I can still remember those Burma Shave signs along the road on the way home. There were six of them, one right after the other that said;

Slow down Pa

Sakes alive

Ma missed signs

Four

And five

Burma Shave

1 Samuel 17:50 "So David prevailed over the Philistine with a sling and with a stone, and smote the Philistine, and slew him; but there was no sward in the hand of David."

DAM DIVING

The old swimming hole at the base of Hinckley Lake Dam had become my favorite summer haven for several years. I would ride my red Schwinn bike, with the big white balloon tires, down the soft, gravel road to the Lake in Metropolitan Park. There was a paved road on either side of the lake that led to both the dam and the swimming hole.

'There was also a bridal path that ran along the edge of the water on each side all the way to the dam. Having lots of twists and turns, it took about a half hour to navigate the trails, giving me four routes from which to choose. Each route had its own unique adventures awaiting as you will soon discover.

At the very base of the dam was what we affectionately called "the old swimmin' hole". It had a concrete floor that stretched out from the base of the dam about fifty feet.

Then the floor turned to light gravel and sand which extended to a smaller two-foot-high dam made of stone. The water a the base of the dam was approximately eight feet deep and the center of the pool was only about five feet in depth. A rope with floats attached, extended about a hundred yards across the middle of the pool. This was a warning for all swimmers to stay away unless they were very strong swimmers. The height of the spillway was about thirty feet and off limits for boating and swimming.

To good swimmers and divers, "OFF LIMITS" was a temptation too exciting to avoid.

Even the trained lifeguards were known to sneak up there and jump or dive into the pool below which was only eight feet deep with a concrete bottom which could be very dangerous. The braces for the dam were angled concrete on each side, from the pool to the top of the dam giving us a graduated platform to work our way to the top. No "off limits" there!

I was almost twelve that summer and hadn't hit my sudden growth spurt yet, I could swim like a fish and had no fear of heights. Diving from the ten-foot diving board was getting too easy and my guard friends were secretly diving from the dam against all the rules. So I, in my infinite stupidity, had to try this death-defying feat.

I climbed the hill next to the dam and slipped over the guard rail with the big "DO NOT GO BEYOND THIS POINT" sign. The spillway only had a drizzle of water going over it since it hadn't rained for the past week. Edging my way out about twenty feet before looking down, I could hear the lifeguards yelling at me to go back and get off that blankety-blank dam! Too late. I was on a mission and I had to complete it. My mind switched gears to overdrive as I remembered some basic facts: thirty feet to the water, only eight feet deep, scattered gravel on a concrete bottom.

What was I doing here? Some people in a nearby rowboat yelled out and offered to pick me up but, this was not an option in my mind. Glaring down at the water below in absolute fear; should I jump or dive? The jump sounded good. Should I sit on the edge and slide off? No. Too close to the wall. I had to jump way out, so jumping made sense. OK, on 3!!! One, two, wait a minute! More thoughts ran through my head. This is stupid! I could really break a leg when I hit the bottom, but if I dive, I could smash my head. Now what??? 1 looked to my left and saw, Johnny Turney, my lifeguard friend, walking toward me. He had jumped from here before. I had watched him do it. To my surprise, he was calm and cool when he walked to my side and said, "Chill out, I'll go with you." "On the count of three." "Keep your feet together and body straight and when you hit the bottom, bend your legs and roll just like jumping off a roof."

He had a way of calming me down and I suddenly felt a spurt of confidence, I looked straight ahead, leaned forward, and together, on three, leaped into the sky. For a moment, felt like a big graceful bird in flight; then I could feel the sting on the bottom of my feet as they struck the surface of the water. Suddenly, my feet and then my hip hit the hard floor of the pool with tremendous force. The next thing I remembered was scrambling toward the surface gasping for air. I exploded through the water like a great white whale and let out a blood-curdling yell. "I did it!"

Now it was time to pay the piper. Standing at the water's edge, the guard supervisor read us the "Riot Act" after determining that we were alright. I was banned from the pool for a week and Johnny got two days off without pay. Was it worth it? You bet! For me it was one more giant step toward manhood. For Johnny, however, it was an unwanted vacation. I never did that again. I know now that God was watching over me and it was meant to be yet another of the many lessons in life that we all have to learn.

Psalms 119:9-10 "Wherewithal shall a young man cleanse his way? by taking heed thereto according to thy word. With my whole heart have I sought thee: O let me not wander from thy commandments."

Romans 11:30 "For as ye in times past have not believed God, yet have now obtained mercy through their unbelief:"

Psalms 71:1-3 "In thee, O Lord, do I put my trust: let me never be put to confusion. Deliver me in thy righteousness, and cause me to escape: incline thine ear unto me, and save me. Be thou my strong habitation, whereunto I may continually resort: thou hast given commandment to save me; for thou art my rock and my fortress.

This is the Hinckley Lake Dam and Swimmin' Hole. Guard stand on the left. There was a diving board in the center and about seven feet of water below.

LOSING A FRIEND

The summer of 1953 was not all fun and frolic. The "old swimming hole" at the base of Hinckley Lake Dam was a summer haven for fun and adventure, usually! But something happened that summer that was horrible and would stick in my memory forever. First, let me relate a little background so that you can fully understand this painfully true story.

The cool, inviting spillway below the dam formed a small lake that was part of the Hinckley Park system and was designated as a public swimming pool. The Metropolitan Parks' Police Chief hired Certified Life Guards to oversee the safety of the swimmers in that area. Each one was Red Cross Certified and very good at what they did. Seventeen-year-old Robert (Bobby) Gettemy was one of those guards; a very strong swimmer and played on the high school football team. Being an eleven-year-old kid that liked to swim, I became good friends with all the guards that summer; and Bobby's sister Ellen was in my class at Hinckley Elementary School.

Bobby walked a two-and-a-half mile trip from his home to the pool each day, and this was a short-cut cross country, that covered dusty corn fields, woods, and ravines with heavy underbrush. On this particular day he had planned to go fishing in the upper lake after his work on the guard stand was finished. Bobby never returned home that evening. He was last seen at the guard locker room where his neatly folded clothes, his fishing pole, and can of fresh worms were found still in his locker.

State and local police, aided by about fifty men and two dozen boy scouts searched the area for fifteen days. The lake was dragged and bloodhounds were brought in, but he was nowhere to be found. Bob sometimes wandered away after a seizure and his parents thought he might try to visit his sister in South Carolina, so the police put out a five state alert. After a week of futile searching without any results, out of a parents' desperation, Rob's dad contacted a known psychic. She told him that she saw Bob in a big lake and that is where Bob's body came up; in the very spot she predicted. He had been caught under some trees close to the middle of the lake where the nets had to be lifted because of the trees and roots when that part of the lake was being dragged.

The psychic also told his parents that there would be a bad storm before Bob was found. Strangely enough, the night before his body came up there was a terrific summer storm. People that lived near the lake said that the water rocked and churned like they had never seen. The next morning Bob's body was discovered floating on the calm water.

On the lake above the dam was a boat dock used for canonists and boaters visiting the pool area to dock their boats. As part of the search team of scouts, I launched boats from there every day. This was the first time I had ever faced the possibility of losing a friend or relative and I was so sure he would come walking up to see what all the fuss was about, just like Tom Sawyer.

About mid-afternoon on the fifteenth day, I was standing about twenty feet from the dock when I saw a search boat heading in my direction. The officer on board called for everyone to stay away from the deck, that they had found the body and were coming ashore. Someone, I don't know who, came up and turned me away to keep me from seeing the remains, but I'll never forget the feeling of realizing that I had just lost a good friend forever.

We later found out that Bobby was prone to epileptic seizures and it was a seizure that, in all possibility, caused him to fall into the lake. He was a great kid and a good friend that I looked up to, but God had other plans for him. At some time in our lives we all face that first time of losing someone to God, and we can all relate and remember as if it were yesterday.

Psalms 107:28-31 "Then they cried out to the Lord in their trouble; and he brought them out of their distress. He stilled the storm to a whisper; the waves of the aca were hushed. They were glad when it grew calm, and he guided them to their desired haven. Let them give thanks to the Lord for His unfailing love and His wonderful deeds for man."

John 3:16 "For God so loved the world, that he gave his only begotten Son, that whosoever believeth in him should not perish, but have everlasting life."

Romans 8:38-39 "For I am persuaded, that neither death, nor life, nor angels, nor principalities, nor powers, nor things present, nor things to come, nor height, nor depth, nor any other creature, shall be able to separate us from the love of God, which is in Christ Jesus our Lord."

Thank you to my friend, classmate, and Bob's sister, Ellen, for her input in this chapter. She and her family love and miss Bob so very much, but know he was a hero and friend to many young kids who shared their summers at the "old swimmin' hole".

This is the dock above the dam where they brought Bobby's
body to shore.

THE DRUM MAJOR

During the summer of '56, I was in a transition period from elementary school to high school. In the Medina County School System at that time they had no middle schools and four-year high schools. They also consolidated some of the elementary schools into one high school class. So that fall I was to become a freshman at Highland High, the land of the Highland Hornets. My brother was a rising senior there. This was a big step to adulthood and I was ready for the challenge. Dick was on the football team and very popular, so he became my mentor. I wanted to be just like him.

I don't know what sidetracked me that summer, but some of my classmates convinced me that because of my height, six feet, I would make a good drum major. They had a special training program at the school and these four girls wanted me to learn to twirl a baton and lead them in some competition scheduled later that summer. Pressured by four really cute girls, I agreed to join them in their quest.

We had six lessons before the competition to learn how to twirl and march to a routine. This was probably the worst decision I had ever made at that stage in my life. We were awful! I would throw the twirling baton high and go look for it. Sometimes I would actually catch it, but usually by accident. This was going to be the low point in my athletic life. The big Saturday come and we all met at the school to be carried to the competition in Medina.

When we arrived, there were groups from all over the state, in all kinds of fancy uniforms, warming up to compete in each respective category. Our girls had sort of matching skirts and blouses and I had on a white shirt and black slacks. We waited three hours for our turn to perform. Our trainer took the record of the music to the stand. We were announced on the loudspeaker and the recording started. Whistle in mouth and high stepping as best I could, off we went to make complete fools of ourselves. The girls were actually pretty good and they did their routines fairly well. I, on the other hand, was a fish out of water.

My first ariel went well. Just to make sure I didn't drop the baton. I only threw it about two feet in the air. Perfect! We turned left and right a couple of times and I had to do another ariel. Confident after the first throw, I let it fly. The girls were behind me concentrating on their moves when I turned to look for my baton. Down it came, hitting one of the girls in the back sow. She stumbled and fell, losing her baton and mine. She found her baton and scrambled to her feet. I left mine on the ground and arched on as if nothing was wrong. I could hear the laughing and giggling coming from the sidelines. What a disaster!!! We marched straight off the field and quickly melted into the crowd. That ended our baton twirling cares forever. At that moment, I committed my future sports adventures to football.

Shortly after our disaster, they had the awards presentation for our classification and trophies were distributed for first, second, and third places. We were shocked when they announced our team as winners of the third-place trophy. The trophy stood about 24 inches high including the majorette on top. "Third Place - Division 4 -Medina County Marching Competition - 1956" Wow!!! I represented the team and went up and received our trophy to loud applause. How could this happen after the poor performance we had? We rode back to our school feeling pretty good. Not bad for our first try. Someone put the trophy in the high school trophy case and there it stayed for about ten years. Every time the girls and I passed it, we grinned and remembered the pact we had made on the way home from the competition. No one was EVER to know that there were only three competitors in our division that day. By the way, I left the girl's names out on purpose. I'm sure they will thank me for that.

Proverbs 11:13 "A talebearer revealeth secrets: but he that is of a faithful spirit concealeth the matter."

THE LEGENDARY LEDGES

A fifteen-minute bike ride from our farm, and part of the Metropolitan Park System, was a special place called "Whipp's Ledges". This was a topical area of rock ledges and crevasses that stretched about a mile along a hillside about 350 feet above the lake and was formed more than 250 million years ago. There was a picnic pavilion at the base and foot trails leading up the hillside to the rock walls and caves above.

In the summer, I would wander these cliffs for hours and came to know every rock and crevice. During the summer of '54, being the entrepreneur that I was, I decided to appoint myself "a guide" and take people on tours of this magnificent natural creation. I made up names for different locations and created stories to go with them.

Among my favorites, was the story I created about a natural stairway between two sheared rocks that was about 60 feet long and rose approximately 40 feet, which became "Jacob's Stairway". This was the place where a warring tribe, the Senecas, ambushed their enemy, the Wyandotte. As they chased them up the stairway, the Seneca warriors sealed off both ends of the stairway and massacred the helpless Wyandotte braves. The hikers really thought that this was a really special place.

Another place I made fascinating was named "The Bear Cave". It was an actual cave that wandered aimlessly through the hill and came out about a half mile away. It actually did, but a cave-in two years earlier sealed the cave off about a hundred feet down the crawlway. This was the home of one of the biggest, meanest, black bears in history. To become a Wyandot warrior, or maybe even a chieftain, a young brave had to spend a night alone in the cave with both entrances guarded. Legend has it that 15 braves entered one year and never came out. Horrible sounds were reported to have rung through the surrounding pine trees causing many sleepless nights for other young braves.

Some of the cliffs along the ridge rose up to 50 feet high and trappers, who had traveled out west, taught the local tribesmen how to herd deer and other game over these cliffs to their death and the waiting squaws below who skinned and prepared them on the spot. The trappers learned this skill from the buffalo hunters and western tribes of the Shawnee and Pone.

On weekends, hundreds of city folk would migrate to the park to enjoy some of mother nature's finest work. A little embellishment, on my part, just added to the excitement of the day. My audience loved it and that was all that mattered to me. "Believe It or Not."

It had to be true. No twelve-year-old kid could make this stuff up, could he? I got as much as a dollar for my efforts which wasn't bad for 1954.

Ecclesiastes 3:12 "I know that there is no good in them, but for a man to rejoice, and to do good in his life."

Galatians 6:9 "And let us not be weary in well doing: for in due season we shall rap, if we faint not."

This is the cave I called the Bear Cave in my story.

The Ledges are still there and visited by thousands of people every year.

Jacob's Stairway hasn't changed much in 50 years.

SOUNDS OF A SUMMER'S NIGHT

Remembering back to those warm summer nights as a child growing up in the country, I can't help but compare the sounds we heard then to the sounds kids hear today, in the city.

As I turned out the lights, tucked myself between my cool summer sheets, and just laid there listening; I was lulled to sleep by the many sounds drifting through the open window. There was usually a cool breeze that delivered clean, fresh air into my room and riding that breeze were sounds that are still etched in my memory today. There was a symphony of crickets, tree frogs, and locusts blending with the occasional hoot of a distant owl while the cool breeze rustled the leaves of the big maples in the front yard. Sometimes a mosquito would sneak in and try to interrupt the relaxing sounds by circling my ear like an airplane waiting to land and taxi to my eardrum. Some nights you could hear distant thunder and see a flicker of distant lightning, but that usually turned out to be a lightning bug that found its way through the open window.

Compare that experience from the farm to the sounds kids hear today should they be brave enough to open a window. The dead, stale air carries in different sounds; automobile horns blaring, police and emergency sirens screaming their way to another accident, neighbors arguing, squealing tires, and an occasional gunshot. In the 40's and 50's, about 80% of the population lived in peaceful rural areas, whereas, today about 80% live in the cities. Now, as I reflect back, I can really appreciate my parents even more for making the sacrifice to move from the convenience of the city to the luxury of the country and a much better way of life.

We didn't have much money back then, but we were richer then any family in the world, because we had love, peace, respect, security, values, friends, and everyday adventures that were all priceless. I had loving parents, friendly neighbors, wonderful school mates and teachers, and most important, a relationship with God that 95% of the people on this orb wish they could have, or really don't know what they are missing, and that relationship prevails to this day. Thank you God for a wonderful country life!

Proverbs 11:28 "He that trusteth in his riches shall fall: but the righteous shall flourish as a branch."

Psalms 118:24 "This is the day which the Lord hath made; we will rejoice and be glad in it."

Ephesians 5:20 "Giving thanks always for all things unto God and the Father in the name of our Lord Jesus Christ."

THE ARMCHAIR
SCOUTMASTER

O ur scout troop, #263, was based out of Parma South Presbyterian Church in Parma Heights, Ohio, and was about a twenty-five-mile drive from the farm to the church. Every Monday night. Dad would drive home from downtown Cleveland, thirty-five miles, pick Dick and me up, and drive back to our scout meetings. That alone was a major task. The greatest part of our scouting adventure, however, was not the scout meetings, but what we affectionately called The Blazak Scout Ranch.

Our property was shaped like a pencil and extended about a half mile back from the road. Through a couple of fields and near the back of the property was an area we designated as "The Campgrounds". Dad cleared the area and the scouts erected a flagpole in the center. Every weekend, spring, summer, and fall, one of the Boy Scout troops from the Cleveland area would come out and camp. Our troop would be there about once a month. I could write a book about just the adventures we had at "The Campgrounds. I'll just tell you a couple so I don't spoil my next book.

The Tenderfoot is the first rank in scouting. As the new boys arrived for their first campout, they had to be initiated. 'The ritual was simple: Catch him, take his pants, and run them up the flagpole. Another method was to teach him how to hunt "Snipes". Snipes are small birds that run along the ground at night and respond to a strange chirping sound that there is no word for. We gave the Tenderfoot a potato sack and had him hide in the bushes, usually far from the camp, and make this weird sound, in hopes that a snipe might hear it and run into the sack. Then, of course, we'd leave him to find his way back; without a snipe, since they are not a native bird to Ohio, or anywhere else.

One more ritual I'll tell you about was the special Mohawk Chiefs Induction. This factitious chief had three gods that he spoke to each night. Their names were: Owa, Tagoo, and Siam. They were the gods of hunting, fishing, and planting. Each night he would face the West and chant their names faster and faster until they answered. The new boys were instructed to do this before the troop until they got their answer. Of course, they had to bow to the west each time they called out the names. Owa-tagoo-siam. Try it, faster and faster, and they will answer.

My dad, the scoutmaster, had wonderful teaching skills as well as a great sense of humor, so he usually watched over our pranks and made sure nothing got out of hand. He also had some great assistant scoutmasters who taught us a lot and told fascinating stories. His low-key approach earned him the title of "The Armchair Scoutmaster"; also because he would have a fold-up armchair outside his tent where he would oversee the camp and our activities.

One thing I want to mention here is Dads dedication to his boys on Sunday morning. He personally cleared a small area in the woods near the campground and, with logs, built a small amphitheater for church. He led us all in beautiful songs that floated through the hardwoods to the heavens. My favorite was "The Little Church in the Wildwood". God had to smile when he heard those campers singing their hearts out on those special Sunday mornings. He was loved and respected by hundreds of boys from all over Ohio. That's my "Pop". He passed on June 5, 2004, at the ripe old age of 94.

Job 8:21 "Till he filthy mouth with laughter, and thy lips with rejoicing."

1 Corinthians 16:18 "For they have refreshed my spirit and yours: therefore acknowledge ye them that are such."

Romans 15:32-33 "That I may come unto you with joy by the will of God, and may with you be refreshed. Now the God of peace be with you all. Amen."

Sign on a church bulletin board on Father's Day: "It's not flesh and blood, but the heart that makes Fathers and Sons."

"The Armchair Scoutmaster"
at one of the many scout Jamborees we attended.

We were a true scouting family.
Three "Eagles" and one " Dove"

CYCLING

In the summer of 1955, I was working feverishly to complete my requirements for the rank of Eagle Scout needing 21 merit badges, some required and some optional. One option, that I had targeted, was the Cycling Merit Badge. The requirements were fairly simple. First, take five twenty-five-mile rides and write a report on each. Second, was to take one fifty-mile ride and complete it in less than ten hours and write a report on it.

Dad, always ready to help, took me in his car straight toward Cleveland on route 44, so that we could mark off a point about 14 miles from the house to the driveway of the Parmadale Orphanage as a turn-around point. Since Dad was the Scoutmaster and tough merit badge counselor, we always had to do a little more than the normal requirements so that no one would think we had it easy. The first five miles of the trip were on a gravel road, which was really tough with my heavy, balloon-tired, Schwinn bike. There were also a number of steep hills that had to be walked, pushing the big, ole" dinosaur along. The rest of the way was not too bad and the traffic was light.

At about the twelve-mile marker, there was a little general store that was like an oasis, a place to stop and rest. The owner was in his early 50s and a former scout who also knew my dad; so naturally Dad saw to it that the owner looked out for me. I would stop and get a Nehi (pronounced "knee high") Orange Soda and Twinkies and listen to hundreds of stories of the olden days when scouting was much tougher.

For six Saturdays in a row that summer, I loaded my canteen with water, my pockets with candy and toilet paper, and headed off on my mission. The weather was always good, and it never rained those Saturdays, but it was really hot and humid. Since I had no time limit on the first five rides, I would stop and goof off along the way; throwing stones at water spiders in the culverts, watching those big ugly buzzards circle, trying my luck at hitting a squirrel with my slingshot, or just laying on a grassy knoll next to the road, watching the clouds roll by.

The final trip was the 50-mile ride to Parmadale and back twice in ten hours or less; but, since I had taken my time on the first five trips, I had no idea how long it really took to go those extra 25 miles. Sometimes I would leave at 9 o'clock in the morning and get back at 4 in the afternoon. This time I had to keep an eye on my watch, keep moving and not dilly-dally along the way. I was up and ready to take off at about 8:00 a.m. I pushed and rode the first lap in 3 hours and 10 minutes. "Cool! This is going to be a breeze." I thought.

I lay around the house and cooled off for about 30 minutes and headed off for my second and final run. As I started pushing the monster up the second gravel ill, I noticed it had gotten heavier and the gravel seemed softer. I had to make several rest stops along the way and by the time I approached the final hill, I was huffing and puffing and drenched with perspiration. When I eventually reached the general store, my canteen was empty and I was ready to drop from exhaustion. After about a 15-minute rest and a   refilled canteen, I pushed on. So much for the easy ride. I was at about the five-hour mark already and not even halfway to my destination. My legs were starting to ache as I reached the store on my final return. It seemed like the remainder was a downhill ride and began to regain my confidence.

I rode like the wind over the paved road and actually gained some time. When I reached the gravel road I was at the eight-hour mark with only about five miles to go. What I had forgotten was that hills go both ways and I was back on gravel. Then the unexpected happened. The bike's chain came off! Rolling the bike over so it sat on the handlebars and seat, I feverishly tried to put that pesky chain back on, and it took a good fifteen minutes to fix it. Off again and behind on time already, a few minutes later, trouble reared its ugly head again. Now with my house in sight, less than a quarter mile away, the rear tire went flat as a pancake! I had twenty minutes to get myself and it, by now, 100-pound bike to the house.

As I looked up the road, I could see my whole family sitting in the front yard cheering me on. They were sitting in lawn chairs, drinking cold stuff, and having a grand old time. I, on the other hand, was beyond exhaustion, dusty, dirty, thirsty, a bike with a flat tire and 200 yards of gravel hills between me and my merit badge. Not to mention I was at the nine-hour and forty-five-minute mark with only 15 minutes to spare.

I don't know how I managed to cover those 200 yards, but I drug that Sherman Tank into the drive with ninety seconds to spare. Collapsing in a tired heap, I shared the cool grass with the three giant maple trees in the front yard for a very long time that evening. Mom produced the coldest, wettest, watermelon I had ever had and we all celebrated my conquest over the seemingly impossible. I think I grow up a little that day, realizing that if you really want something badly enough, you can do amazing things to get it.

Proverbs 24:16 "For the just man falleth seven times, and riseth up again: but the wicked shall fall into mischief."

2 Timothy 4:7 "I have fought a good fight, I have finished my course, I have kept the faith."

Ruth 2:12 "The Lord recompense thy work, and a full reward be given thee of the Lord God of Israel, under whose wings thou art come to trust."

Philippians 4:6-7 "Be careful of nothing; but in every thing by prayer and supplication

with thanksgiving let your requests be made known unto God. And the peace of God, which passeth all understanding, shall keep your hearts and minds through Christ Jesus."

THE FALL

GREEN APPLES AND APPENDICITIS

Next to the house and near the road was a wonderful orchard with a variety of fruit trees; apple, pear, plum, peach, and cherry. The old apple tree near the driveway was the biggest tree in the orchard and had ideal limbs for climbing. Dick and I decided it was the best tree in which to build a tree fort. Rounding up scraps of lumber from here and there, hammers, and an assortment of nails we proceeded to construct a masterpiece to make Frank Lloyd Wright proud.

After about three weekends of diligent labor and bruised thumbs, we were ready to move in. There was just enough room on the floor for our two sleeping bags, hooks on the walls for the lanterns, a long rope for quick escapes, and a roof of odd-shaped plywood scraps. The one unique feature of our new pad was its unlimited supply of ripe, juicy, apples. We also had our canteens filled with Cherry Kool-Aid to protect us from dehydration. Our first night was pretty uneventful except for a few overzealous mosquitoes and bees. The next day was a Saturday and we had things to do, so we left our tree house for other adventures.

At about noon that hot, sunny Saturday, I started feeling a little sick to my stomach and the pain began to get worse. Complaining to my mother, I was given some Milk of Magnesia and told to go to my bedroom and lie down for an hour. After an hour, the pain had gotten worse, to the point of tears. I couldn't even stand upright without grabbing my stomach and crawling back on the bed to get into a more comfortable fetal position.

Mom knew that I had no reason to fake an illness and something was definitely wrong so she loaded me into the car and we were off to the ER. Saturday was not a good day to see the doctor, and that hasn't changed in the last 50 years.

Upon arriving at the emergency room at Medina Hospital, we sat and filled out papers for what seemed like hours, while I begged for relief. That hasn't changed either. Finally, a doctor came by and questioned me on my food intake over the previous twenty-four hours and I told him about the apples I had eaten the day before. Since the apples I had eaten were green, even though they were ripe, the doctor determined that this was the cause of the stomach pain. He arranged to have my stomach pumped to eliminate the problem, but an hour later I was in serious distress and my temperature had started to spike. A second doctor took one look at me and ordered an x-ray of my stomach and intestinal area to confirm his concern that it might be something more serious than green apples, causing the pain.

Minutes later, I was hooked up to all kinds of tubes, needles were stuck in my arm and then the lights went out. I was rushed to the operating room where my appendix was removed, and we learned later that my appendix actually burst while I was on the operating table. If they delayed ten minutes longer, the poison from the infected appendix could have spread into my body and I could have died. Had my mom not understood my pain, and had that second doctor not stepped in when he did, I might not be writing this book today. God does work in mysterious ways. He has a plan for us and our future is in His hands. Of course, you knew that, didn't you?

LYRICS FROM A POPULAR SONG OF THE SAME NAME: "God is watching you from a distance."

Psalms 126:3 "The Lord hath done great things for us; whereof we are glad."

My first big business venture.

PAINTING THE ROOF

In the spring of 1954, I had finally turned twelve and Dick was fifteen. The house was slowly evolving into a pretty nice country home. We now had heat, water, and electricity. To the south side of the house, we had added a screened - porch on the front and a big utility room on the back. The kitchen was remodeled to include a big credenza with glass doors to store dishes and stuff and I still remember the Johnny Appleseed wallpaper my mom picked out. The next big project was to build a big bedroom on the north side for my mom and dad. As a young boy, that room seemed like a gymnasium. In later years, when I revisited the farm, it seemed much smaller.

By July, the room was near completion. The new shingles were in place and gutters were installed. On the exterior, the only thing left was to paint the outside wall to which the room was attached. This was the area just above the new roof. My brother was given this project and early one evening, when the temperature had cooled somewhat, he climbed the ladder, with paint bucket and brush in hand, to apply the first coat.

He had worked about a half hour and decided that he had done a superb job. Stepping back to admire his work, he forgot about the paint bucket he had balanced on the peak of the roof behind him. Kicking it with the heel of his grungy high top, the nearly full gallon of white outdoor paint went tumbling down the roof, pouring its contents in all directions. Dick turned quickly and reached to catch the bucket, only to lose his balance and follow it, head first, down the slanted roof. He slid rapidly, gaining speed and gaining on the bucket until there was no more roof. Now airborne, he let out a thundering cry that, I think, resembled "HELP!!". The good news was that the bedroom wing was only one story high. The bad news was that he was leaving it head first, blinded and covered in paint. As he hit the ground, the dirt and grass added to the paint looking if he had just been tarred and feathered. With a bruised arm and ego, he clambered to his feet, only to have the rest of the paint cascade from the roof like a waterfall and cover his already white head.

I was standing nearby and watched the whole thing in true amazement. He turned toward me, wiped the paint from his eyes, and said something that caused me to break into uncontrolled laughter. "Don't tell Dad what happened!!." I looked up at the new roof, half black and half white, and just couldn't contain myself. Then I looked back at Dick, covered from head to toe in paint, spotted with dirt and clumps of grass, and just couldn't hold it back. Realizing the situation and what he had just said, Dick joined me in a special moment of brotherly bonding.

I think, to this day, the back side of the bedroom roof is still two-tone.

• •

Romans 12:9-10 " Let love be without dissimulation, Abhor that which is evil; cleave to that which is good. Be kindly affectioned one to another with brotherly love; in honour preferring one another."

Deuteronomy 22:8   "Win thou buildest a new house, then thou shalt make a battlement for thy roof, that thou bring not blood upon thine house, if any man falls from thence."

GARDEN FRESH

L iving on a farm with limited income, one of the ways to save money was to grow your own food. Our first spring began with what was to become the greatest garden in Ohio. Dad prepared a plot of land near the house and we planted our first real garden. We had, what seemed to me at age 8, about two hundred rows of everything you could imagine. From asparagus to zucchini. This included eggplant, tomatoes, potatoes, sweet potatoes, peas, beans, squash, watermelon, strawberries, pumpkins, field corn, onions, sweet corn, popcorn, lettuce, broccoli, and about ten different kinds of flowers, just to mention a few things. In another area behind the barn, we had a berry patch. This was home to about twenty rows of black and red raspberries. The fields were spotted with large patches of wild blackberries which, thank goodness, were maintenance-free.

The garden chores were the worst. Hand tools had to be used then, so we always employed hoes and garden rakes. All that work paid off in the fall when harvest time began. Mom prepared and canned most of it for the winter, but we had our share while it was still really fresh. I can still remember sitting in the middle of the tomato patch, with a cardboard shaker of Morton Salt, rubbing off the dirt and consuming way too many of those juicy buggers. Today I'd be covered with cold sores from the acid. I still push the limits of my tomato intake.

Dinnertime was so memorable since we had a personal relationship with our food. One of the major food groups was, SPAM. My mom had a hundred ways to cook SPAM and somehow it always tasted good. One recipe is an old family secret called Blazak Stew. This is your lucky day because I'm going to pass it on to you. This will feed two adults, three children, or me. In a saucepan put: one can of diced SPAM, one can of sliced white potatoes, and one can of Campbell's Chicken Noodle Soup. Mix well at low heat and serve with bread and butter and a glass of cold milk. As the stew evolved, I added veggies, mushrooms, and anything else left over in the refrigerator. Sounds awful but give it a chance. At least it's cheap.

The meat, including Spam, came from the local General Store. Ours was Stahl's Grocery, about 5 miles away at Remson's Corners. This was a great little store that had all kinds of food, fresh meat, and vegetables. Also all kinds of candy! They had a big freezer where they could store frozen meat like venison from the deer we shot each fall. We had a big white freezer that opened from the top, in our utility room, where we kept all our frozen foods. We mixed up venison with hamburger to stretch our dollars. This was also the home of a five-gallon container of ice cream that was given out on special occasions. A bakery truck came by about every 10 days and we would freeze about a half dozen loaves of white bread.

Chicken and eggs were never a problem since we lived across the road from Weema's chicken farm. We traded vegetables for them and had all we needed. I've told you all about Garret and his wonderful farm in an earlier chapter.

We ate well and healthy in those days. Not much junk food and most was fresh. No wonder my mom used to say that I would grow out of my clothes before she could get them home from the store. Life was good.

Genesis 1:11-12   "And God said, Let the earth bring forth grass, the herb yielding seed, and the fruit tree yielding fruit after his kind, whose seed is in itself, upon the earth: and it did so. And the earth brought forth grass, and herb yielding seed after his kind, and the tree yielding fruit, whose seed was in itself   after his kind: and God saw that it was good."

2 Corinthians 9:6 "But this I say, He which soweth sparingly shall reap also sparingly; and he which soweth bountifully shall reap also bountifully."

Jeremiah 29:5   "Built ye houses, and dwell in them; and plant gardens, and eat the fruit from them."

This is Dad preparing our first garden in 1949.

HAY! DON'T SMOKE!!!

Every fall it became a tradition to store hay bails in our barn. Mr. Weema supplied most of the bails and Dick and I earned some extra money loading the wagon from the fields and unloading them into the barn. We used bailing hooks that had wooden handles on a big hook that resembled Captain Hook's hook hand. When we stacked the bails in the barn, we would arrange them so we created tunnels and rooms like an ant hill throughout the stack. We would crawl through these tunnels and hide from each other. I remember one section leads to a small room with wood planks for a roof and soft hay on the floor. Since it was pitch black, strangers would blindly crawl through and suddenly fall three feet to their deaths. One tunnel went along the side of the barn and we rigged a board so we could twist it and sneak out leaving our guests lost for weeks.

Dick was 16 in the fall of 1956 and in Highland High School. Since he was "all grown up" and bulletproof, he decided to do something totally forbidden by man. Smoke a cigarette. His first mistake was smoking at all. His second mistake was trying it in the barn. His third mistake was trying it sitting in a stack of loose hay with my sister and me, and the really big mistake was getting caught by Dad. Loose hay creates tons of dust that is highly combustible and, of course, the dry hay would basically explode from one small spark.

There we sat, about 10 feet off the barn floor with no quick escape, watching my brother about to light a match when in walked Dad. He looked up and let out a yell that I remember to this day. "Don't light that!!!!!" One second later and we could have all been incinerated. "All of you get down here right now!!", he shouted.

We all got the lecture of our lives. My dad was furious. I never saw him that angry before. After scolding Sue and me profusely, he turned to Dick, removed his belt, and for the first and only time in his life, whipped Dick on his backside about 3 times. I know that later, both felt very badly about what had happened, but the upside is that none of us, to my knowledge, ever lit another cigarette.

I looked back on my family history and realized that longevity is a family trait. Mom and Dad both passed away at the age 94. Had we picked up that bad habit, who knows how many wonderful years we would have lost? Thanks to God's timing, we are all still here, healthy and a lot smarter.

PROVERBS 22:6 "Train up a child in the way he should go: and when he is old, he will not depart from it."

WINTER WONDERLAND

IGLOOS IN OHIO?

During the winter, there were lots of occurrences related to our location with respect to Lake Erie. When snow storms came in from Canada, they would sweep across the lake and as they reached the big City of Cleveland, the heat from the population and all the concrete would cause the air to rise above the buildings; then as it moved into the suburbs and on into the countryside it would dump snow by the foot. This was called the Snow Belt and stretched all the way to Buffalo, New York. We used to listen to the weather forecast on Radio Station WHK and if the weatherman predicted three to four inches in the city, we prepared ourselves for three to four feet in the country where we lived. Every winter in Hinckley was a winter wonderland. Dad knew most of the scoutmasters in Cleveland and would invite them to bring their Boy Scout troops to the farm for winter camping on weekends.

My dad, my brother, and I had studied the Eskimo Indian lore books on igloo making and tried our hand at building several in the backyard. We would roll large snowballs, then take a shovel and cut them into blocks. Starting with a good, large round base, we stacked circles smaller and smaller until we had just a small hole left for the smoke to escape through the top of the dome-shaped igloo. Spraying it with water would add strength, but it was usually so cold already that we skipped that part.

The boys arrived on Saturday morning, pulling toboggans and sleds and transporting their camping gear to the campsite, located in a grove of trees about a quarter mile from the house. Out of the barn would come the infamous Ford-Ferguson tractor. That thing could go anywhere, in any terrain and once everyone had arrived, we would tie all the sleds and toboggans in a long train, load them down with all the gear, and let the tractor do the rest.

The boys marked off their locations by sticking tree branches in the snow and began the task of building what was to be their home for the night. It had to be big enough to allow two boys to spread out their sleeping bags and still have room to build a fire in the center. They also needed space to store their gear and the all-important firewood.

I remember how some of the boys, wishing to finish in a hurry, thus lacking patience, would build too small or too thin, causing the roof to cave in prematurely. We usually took an old Army tent back to them so they wouldn't have to sleep outside. With a central bonfire to sit around, those cold, clear, starry nights were etched in our hearts and minds forever. You may wince at the thought of sitting outside in the cold at night, but for a young city boy, it was truly an adventure.

One cold, snowy weekend in January of 1955 a group of Explorer Scouts from Berea, these were senior Scouts between 14 and 18 years old, arrived for their winter adventure; four boys under the age of 16 along with their dads. In those days, dads seemed to get more involved with their sons' activities. One of the dads, the Post leader (similar to a Scoutmaster), had to stay behind to work, but would join his son, Josh, that evening.

Josh was one of the two Eagle Scouts in that Troop, a great kid, a good leader, and had earned numerous awards throughout his scouting years. He was a member of the Order of the Arrow, had his Eagle with Three Palms, and the God and Country Award from his church. His dad was there to encourage him all the way. Standing about 5'8", he was a proud example of the kind of young man scouting was designed to create. Besides being straight. A student and a great baseball player, he worked part-time in a record store. What stood out this day was Josh's engineering abilities.

We had a heavy snowfall that week and the campground had about three feet of the fluffy white stuff with drifts as high as six feet. Josh was prepared with a plan to have his igloo ready by the time his dad arrived, so he could just climb in and relax. After laying out his floor plan, Josh went to work, and by the end of the day, had built the most impressive igloo any of us had ever seen. It would have made any Eskimo proud. The center of his igloo was over seven feet high with the fireplace in the middle, carefully surrounded with stones to contain the fire. There were small windows or peek-holes cut in the walls in order to see out and let the air flow properly, keeping the smoke flowing up the chimney hole. He had also, lined the floor with plastic to keep the gear and sleeping bags dry.

Very late in the afternoon, almost completed, he sprinkled the exterior of his masterpiece with creek water to give it extra strength and finished it off with a six-foot tunnel to the door to keep out the wind. Using a stick, he even highlighted the bricks on the exterior by outlining each one. His dad was due to arrive about 6 o'clock and in addition to building the igloo, he prepared dinner fit for a king. Everything was ready right on schedule and when his dad arrived as promised, my dad and I led him back to the campsite where they greeted each other with a hug, and the pride in his son showed in his father's eyes.

As darkness set in the temperature quickly dropped to 10 degrees and the igloos turned into huge blocks of solid ice. Josh had created a masterpiece but had made one major mistake. The tunnel' His dad was 6'5" tall, weighed around 265 pounds, and there was not a shoe horn big enough that would help him fit into that tunnel. To this day, I can still see the disappointment on Josh's face when he realized his error in his calculations for the tunnel.

I often wonder where Josh is today and how his future developed. I'm sure he is very successful, maybe an engineer somewhere, but for sure, a real asset to our country. Scouting plus parenting equals almost guaranteed success.

Childhood memories like these will last a lifetime; not just for me, but for every boy that visited The Blazak Scout Ranch. Summer and winter hundreds of young boys developed many different skills, built unforgettable memories and learned things about life and nature that would help shape their futures and the rest of their lives.

Proverbs 4:1-3   "Hear, ye children, the instruction of the father, and attend to know understanding. For I give you good doctrine, forsake ye, not my law. For I was my father's son, tender and only beloved in the sight of my mother."

Psalms 19:12   "Who can understand his errors? Cleanse thou me from secret faults."

SLEDS VS. ANTHILLS

As kids, one of the fun winter sports was called "Taxi". The object of the game was to belly slam onto our sleds, side by side, and careen down a hill at breakneck speeds. Whoever got to the bottom first was the winner. The catch, however, was to arrive at the bottom alone.

Not far from the house was the perfect hill. At the bottom was the Artesian spring from where we got our drinking water. One sunny, but chilly, day during Christmas break, my brother and I decided to challenge each other to a race. We had great sleds. They were wood with metal rails and steering systems and about four feet long. We waxed the runners with old candles to get maximum speed. My big brother always won these races, but I kept trying my best to outride him.

The night before, mother nature had left a nice 6 inches of fresh snow gently covering the hill. Not a mark on it; smooth and fast. We called out the countdown and dashed toward the crest of the hill, landing simultaneously and darting downward. I swerved next to him and got onto my hands and knees. This was my chance. I leaped onto his back and began tugging on his coat. At that very moment, his sled hit a hidden ant hill and went airborne. Also, at that same moment, my brother turned and buried his elbow firmly into my left cheek.

Now I was airborne, landing face down on the hillside and sliding feet first toward the bottom of the hill. As I clawed myself to a stop, I lifted my head to see where I was. My coat had what seemed like a ton of snow packed in it, but before I could react, something struck me with the force of a train. It was my empty sled with its metal steering bar across the front. Right across the forehead, causing a gash about six inches long and knocking me out cold. Blood was pouring onto the snow, which looked like gallons to my brother.

In a panic, he ran for the house. Stumbling into the back mud room, he yelled for Mom. " I think I just killed Bob!", I'm told he yelled.

My mom, all five feet of her and coatless, ran to my aide. By the time she got to me, I was conscious and screaming bloody murder. She knew what to do. She was my morn. Using a scarf as a compress, she controlled the bleeding and calmed me down. Once I stopped blubbering like a baby, she lovingly walked me back to the house and called our neighbor. My dad was at work and mom didn't drive, so our good neighbor with the chicken farm across the road, Mr. Weema, came to the rescue.

He rushed over in his old station wagon. He used it to deliver his eggs to the city. Off we went to Medina Hospital where we were greeted like old friends. Seems like they knew us on a first-name basis there. By the time you finish this book, you'll understand why.

The lesson here is simple. Don't play "Taxi" with my brother. Check for ant hills first.

PSALM 121 1-2 "I will lift my eyes unto the hills, from whence cometh my help. My help cometh from the LORD, which made the heaven and earth."

BOW HUNTING RABBITS

Living on the farm in the 50s, with a limited income, was much different than they are today. Our food supply came from the large garden planted full of every variety of vegetables, and much of our meat came from the local general store; or on occasion, from deer and pheasants that my dad would bring home from a day of hunting. In the winter of '53 I became interested in archery and, with my Dad's support and guidance, learned everything that I could about bows and arrows, and Indian lore. My dad found a craftsman in Medina that did woodworking and made bows for hunting, and as a surprise, he had one made for himself; Dick, and me. Mine was laminated wood with curled ends, with a 45-pound pull to match my height and weight I learned how to string it by wrapping my leg between the string and the bow, wedging one end behind my foot and pushing on the other end to secure the string. Dad bought me a "fletcher", which is a tool used to attach feathers to an arrow, dowel rods that would become the shafts, and knocks, which were glued to the shafts and the feather end so that the string could hold the arrow when being drawn, and feathers to make my own arrows. I had a wide variety of arrowheads for hunting different kinds of animals. Deer arrowheads were diamond shaped and very sharp. Bird arrowheads were blunt, so they wouldn't stick in the trees but could knock a bird or squirrel to the ground. Fishing points had barbs like a fish hook. (You'll learn more about them in another chapter.) Target arrowheads are what most people see on arrows and are shaped so that they can easily be pulled out of a target.

After about a month of practice, I decided I was ready to help bring in the game for dinner. I was reminded of one very important rule that my dad was really serious about. "You shoot only what you can eat. Be sure of what you're aiming at before you let the strings go." He didn't want us shooting groundhogs, skunks, or cows, and definitely not each other.

There was a light dusting of snow that morning and the fields were covered with animal tracks. I bundled up in my winter gear, buckled up my black, rubber goulashes, slung my quiver of arrows over my shoulder, and headed out on my big adventure. Walking a zig-zag path through the field near the house, I had my bow and arrow ready to draw and fire, but though the field was full of rabbit tracks, they were too fast for a beginner like me.

As I glared ahead something dashed in front of me running from left to right. A full-grown rabbit was on the move and I took aim and fired. Bingo! Right through the neck! He tumbled and fell, flopped a couple of times, and lay dead in the snow. "That guy could feed the whole family tonight.", I thought as I marched proudly over to pick him up. Dad watching the whole incident from the back yard shouted, "Did you get him?" Standing over my trophy, I looked down and swallowed heavily. I was in big trouble. I had just shot one of our cats. "No, I missed." I quickly answered, hoping to somehow cover up my crime. But there was no escape, Dad was already on his way to see what I had shot.

He looked down and saw the cat with the arrow right through the neck "Nice shot! Now you know the rules. You'll have to skin and prepare him for Mom to cook up for dinner. I'll get the hunting knife for you."

He walked off toward the house and I stood there in absolute horror. "This is a cat!!!", I thought "We can't eat a cat, — can we?" Feeling sick to my stomach, I picked it up, pulled the arrow out, and headed for the house, dragging that cat by its hind legs. Dad, followed by Mom, both looking serious, came out of the house with a big hunting knife in hand and met me in the yard. Dad handed me the knife and said, "Start at the neck and.......... " At that point, Mom finally spoke up and said to my Dad, "O.K., that's enough. I think he's learned his lesson. He's starting to turn green." Then turning to me she directed, "Go bury the cat, clean up, and be more careful what you shoot at in the future." I'll never know if Dad would have made me actually prepare that cat for human consumption; I don't think so. In retrospect, I know he wouldn't. I don't think.......... WASTE NOT, WANT NOT!

Genesis 27:34   "Now therefore take, I pray thee, thy weapons, thy quiver and thy bow, and go out to the field, and take me some venison; and make me savoury meat, such as I love, and bring it to me, that I may eat; that my soul may bless thee before I die."

Psalms 130:4 "But there is forgiveness with thee, that thou mayest be feared."

Psalms 11:2   "For lo, the wicked bend their bows, they make ready their arrow upon the string, that they may privily shoot at the upright in heart."

BUZZARD HUNTING

My 12th birthday was a very special one because it was, to me, a big step toward manhood. Living on the farm, we had great respect for all animals, domestic and wild. My dad and brother both owned shotguns that they used for hunting those wild animals that helped put food on the table. There was only one steadfast rule that could absolutely not be broken. You could only shoot games that you could eat; rabbits, turkeys, pheasants, and deer were fair game, but anything else was "off limits".

On the morning of March 23rd, (My birthday!), I was up early and anxious to get my present. I already knew what it was, but the anticipation was still overwhelming. It was a Sunday and my parents decided that my party would be after church and then lunch. I squirmed my way through the morning service and Sunday school and it was around 1:00 o'clock before we arrived back home. Lunch was inhaled quickly and finally, the cake came to the table. Mom made my favorite cake in the whole world; CONFETTI ANGEL FOOD, and after a couple of large pieces, I was ready for the big moment.

Dad came into the room bearing my gift; A Savage, Over-Under. 20 gage. 22 caliber, single-shot, shotgun. rifle. This was no toy, I was reminded as my dad, hero of heroes, and ten feet tall, in my eyes, took me out behind the farthest building and began to set up some targets. He wedged about six corncobs on a fence rail, brought out a large box of shotgun shells and rifle cartridges, and proceeded to instruct me on the proper way to shoot at the target or any wild game. That was another one of the many really special days with my dad that I will never forget; no one but him and me, and my Savage. We must have spent an hour or more out there practicing on that cold and drizzly day, but I never noticed. We used up the whole box of ammo before going in wet and tired, but ecstatic.

I had to wait until the next weekend to use my new gun and only then was I allowed to take it on my first hunting trip alone. This was to be a squirrel hunt in a large densely wooded area, the trees full of squirrels' nests, just beyond the valley where I used to race boats in the creek. Along the way, I passed by the edge of a large hay field coming to the fire trail that was just about ten yards into the wooded area. I walked carefully, alone, with the butt of the gun tucked under my arm, my finger on the trigger, and the safety on, just as Dad had instructed me.

Nearing my wooded goal, I noticed that there were about a half dozen buzzards circling over the field, coming ever closer to me with each circle. Trying to keep an eye out for squirrels, I kept reminding myself that buzzards are harmless birds that only eat dead animals. They are, however, capable of growing to as large as an 8-foot wing span. Suddenly one of the birds broke from the flock and headed in my direction. What I didn't realize was that I was upwind from him and he apparently didn't even see me.

I kept thinking any moment he would see me and fly off to "Birdland" somewhere. That didn't happen. He kept coming. Being 12 and just a little kid, I turned quickly toward him, popped the safety, aimed, and fired. That bird was only about 10 feet from me when he dropped to the ground. He was so close, even my sister could have shot him.

I tip-toed over to him and poked him with the barrel of my gun, which was already reloaded, just in case. His ugly red head flopped back and he still had his wings spread. After my heart started beating again, I took a closer look and gauged his wing spam to be about 20 to 30 feet across. Then I looked next to him and realized what had just happened. There, on a tree stump, was a carcass of a dead field mouse! Being so bundled up with clothes, I apparently didn't give off any scent, but the dead mouse did. Big Bird was just picking up dinner and went to the wrong restaurant.

I headed home that day without any squirrels, but I had just killed my first Pteranodon. Being all too aware of that family hunting rule, "You kill you eat it," I must admit I never told my dad what happened on my first hunting trip.

Genesis 6, 19 – 20   "And of all living thing of all flesh, two of every sort shalt thou bring into the ark, to keep them alive with thee; they shall be male and female. Of fowls after their kind, and of cattle after their kind, of every creeping thing of the earth after his kind, two of every sort shall come unto thee, to keep them alive."

THE FIRST KISS

I started my first school year at Hinckley Elementary as a third grader, and I still remember my teacher, Mrs. Wing. She was, to me at the time, an old, mean lady that always demanded full attention. I recall her getting into trouble one day when "she thought" I was talking out of turn in class and proceeded to discipline me using a wooden dowel that she used as a pointer at the blackboard. (We really did have BLACK boards back then). She instructed me to stand and commenced to smack me on the bottom with her weapon. Not being very coordinated, she caught me right in the small of my back.

That night I felt sick and complained to my mom of severe back pain. I told her what had happened at school that afternoon and the next morning she took me to our family doctor who discovered I had a badly bruised kidney. What I failed to mention was that my mom was a second-grade teacher in the classroom directly across the hall from my class. You don't want to know what this 100 pounds of wildfire could do when upset. Within a week, I actually had a new teacher and became the class hero.

There was a little tomboy in that class, Janet Bartel, who was an instant and cherished friend and still is today. In the third grade, we were earmarked as "boyfriend and girlfriend". She could play baseball and run faster than most of the boys and we were part of a group of about 8 kids who just bonded and are still best friends after all these years.

Now move ahead about 4 years and Janet's mom had invited most of us to their home for   Janet's 12th birthday party in their basement. We had all the trimmings, party hats, cake, music, presents, games, ice cream, etc. I remember George and Dorothy (brother and sister), Linda, Bob, Roger, Richard, Judy, and of course, the birthday girl, Janet were all there. We listened to the current 50's music, but being at that awkward age back then, no one had the nerve to dance. Then, to my horror, someone suggested we play "SPIN THE BOTTLE"! There was no escape, so I slipped away upstairs to the bathroom and stayed as long as I could, but when I returned, they were just beginning. Forming a circle on our knees, we alternated boy, girl and put a Coke bottle in the center. Of course, Janet, being the hostess, got the first spin. I tried to make myself as small as possible, hoping the bottle would not see me, but sure enough, it did!

She was my friend and buddy; and sure, she was really cute, but kiss her? No way!!! The next thing I heard was the gang chanting, "KISS HER!" "KISS HER!", "BOBBY HAS TO KISS   JANET!"

Well with all that noise and cheering, I decided to look at it as an athletic challenge, gritted my teeth and went for it. I tried for her cheek, but she outmaneuvered me and I got her right on the lips and my face turned fire engine red! When that embarrassment was finally over, I quickly   retreated to my place in the circle. I figured I'd never live it down, but then everyone else took their turn. My debut was completely overshadowed when George had to kiss his sister. I had no idea that this historical moment was the beginning of a lifetime of kisses and hugs lasting into adulthood and many more memorable moments.

Job 27:3-5 "All the while my breath is in me, and the spirit of God in my nostrils; My lips shall now speak wickedness, nor my tongue utter deceit. God forbid that I should justify you: till I die I will not remove mine integrity from me."

Here's the gang at that party. Janet's at the front right. What a wonderful bunch of friends!

This is Janet and I heading out to represent our Freshman Class at the "May Dance" in 1957.

THE "WALLED-OFF ASSTORIA"

Our first winter had something missing in our farmhouse, - PLUMBING! There was no running water, so we had to make some major adjustments with regard to bathing, drinking water, toilets, and dishwashing.

We had two sources of water: a cistern that collected rain water from the roof and an artesian spring, about 200 yards from the house, that supplied an endless flow of clean, cold drinking water.

Bathing was a major ordeal as the cistern water had to be brought to the kitchen in three-gallon buckets, heated on the gas stove, and poured into a huge galvanized tub in the middle of the kitchen floor. Then, one by one, Dick, Sue, and I would strip down and dive in, with a bar of Swan soap. The soap did it all, as a body cleaner, shampoo, conditioner, and bubble maker. To conserve the hot water, this process had to be done quickly, but we usually dawdled because the warm water felt so good. When done, or when mom said we were done, we'd jump out to a big, soft, bath towel in mom's waiting arms. After we were tucked in bed and reviewed the day with Mom or Dad, we were off to slumber while Mom and Dad took their turn at the big old tub of tepid, sort of clean, soapy water.

Drinking water came from the artesian spring. For hauling it to the house. Dad made a shoulder yoke that would hang two three-gallon buckets. I did most of the hauling of water. We each had our chores and that was my job. I had a reputation for being a little clumsy so by the time I got back to the house, the buckets were usually half full. The drinking water from the spring was kept in a big glass jug in the "fridge" and the rest was heated and used for washing dishes. The real challenge was the bathroom.

This is where the real story begins. We had an outhouse about 100 feet from the house. It was a three-holer and not in the best condition. During that winter we had to shovel a path to it so we could scurry out at night with a flashlight, do our thing and rush back to the warm house. There was no moon cut in the door, but it did have a personality of its own. The hinge on the door was rusted and squeaked, the wood near the floor was rotted away allowing the cold wind to blow in, and it was the winter home of a variety of varmints like opossums, raccoons, skunks, field mice, rats, squirrels, and a few unknown critters of the night. When we approached the building we would wave our flashlights, sing loudly, or stamp our feet, to give them a running start. Often you could see eyes staring at you in the beam of the flashlight. Inside was the usual equipment: a roll of toilet paper, a stick to prop the door shut, and the famous Sears catalog,

During our first spring, Dad had a company come out and dig a well just outside the back door. He installed plumbing throughout the house and the old outhouse was put out of business, so to speak. By the way, Dad did most of the work himself. Being a city slicker, he would sit up nights reading books on how to plumb, build, and farm. There was nothing he couldn't do and he taught us as he learned. The old outhouse sat there as a refuge for critters, wasps, bees, and anything that needed to get out of the weather for about two years until it was moved to the back of the property where the scout campsite was created. Dad uses the tractor to drag it almost a half mile to the backfield. With his backhoe, he dug a big hole and we set the building on it. That summer, the scouts cleaned it up and painted it about four different colors. It needed a name, so we had a contest. The first prize was unique and we painted the name on the outside of the door with a quarter moon under it. To this day, The "Walled-off Asstoria" is still leaning heavily in the woods near the field that was the campground. Now you know the rest of the story.

John Wesley   "Certainly this is a duty, not a sin. Cleanliness is indeed next to Godliness."

James 1:4 "But let patience have her perfect work, that ye may be perfect and entire, wanting nothing."

This is how I carried spring water for drinking. Mom made that Dutch costume for a school play.

I'm actually wearing wooden shoes borrowed from Mrs. Weema across the road.

BUZZARDS AGAIN

I n the winter of 1955, Dick had just turned 16 and, like many 16-year-olds, he got his driver's license the day after his birthday. My mom was teaching second grade at Hinckley Elementary School and after school, she would usually drive us all home in a 1949, black, Chevy coupe that my dad had purchased from a friend of his. It was late March and during the day there was a heavy snowfall covering the recently plowed roads. The route home took us onto State Route 4 which passed through the Metropolitan Park on a gravel road with a steep downhill about a quarter mile long and was bordered by heavy woods.

Mom hated to drive in good weather and when she saw the snow-covered roads, she panicked. Dick, on the other hand, had been driving for weeks and felt confident that he could handle the wintery challenge. Somehow, he convinced Mom that he could safely drive us home in one piece, so off we went. Sue was with us also, as she was a fifth grader at the same school. As we approached the big hill, we could barely see the toboggan run to the right. The snow clung to the trees and bushes and described the roadway, making it difficult to tell where the road actually was.

Moving slowly and trying to see through the semi-frozen windows, all was going well until all of a sudden, right in front of us were, you guessed it, BUZZARDS. About half a dozen big, ugly, buzzards, fresh from their arrival from the south, had gathered to feast on a dead animal right in the middle of the road.

Dick, with all his experience and wisdom, cranked the wheel to the left in an effort to avoid them. Then, overcompensating, jerked the wheel back to the right, putting us into a wild spin. Suddenly we were sailing, BACKWARDS, into the woods. We wound up about 30 feet off the road and wedged firmly between two large maple trees. The trees were inches from both doors of the old coupe and locked us in tightly with no way to open the doors. There we sat with the motor running and buried in snow and mud. Because of the snow and bad roads, there was no traffic to hail down with the horn, so we were really in a pickle.

Fortunately, Sue was with us and we rolled the passenger window down so she could squeeze out and go for help. We were about 2 miles from the house and she bravely trudged through the snow to our good neighbor's farm, Garrett Weema, who again came to our rescue with his tractor and Sue riding shotgun. With chains and patience, he pulled us back to the road and followed us home with no further mishaps. He was getting pretty used to rescuing us individually or in a group. We city slickers were slow to learn. I'm sure those buzzards were nearby laughing at us for losing control and visiting the local woods. The car wound up without a mark on it and no one was hurt, so we had that to be thankful for. Those buzzards may be smarter than we gave them credit for. Just another adventurous day in our winter wonderland.

PSALMS 32: 7   "Thou art my hiding place; thou shalt preserve me from trouble; thou shalt compass me about with songs of deliverance. Selah."

PARTY ON WHEELS

Christmas time at Hinckley Elementary School was always special. The last day before the winter break was set aside for a class party and everyone exchanged gifts, had lots of food and goodies, and the teachers usually got enough apples to last for years. My fourth grade class had just that kind of day planned and I was excited about being a part of it all. I was up early that morning, dressed, and ready to catch the school bus. Mom was teaching at the school and had to leave much earlier and drive to school. The bus would stop in front of the house at precisely 7:00 each morning and when I didn't ride with Mom, I'd catch the bus to school. There was heavy snow the night before and the roads were covered, but this was Ohio and no one worried about a little snow.

Sue had gone with Mom and Dick was picked up by one of his friends, so I was the last to leave. About ten minutes to seven, I was putting on my goulashes, scarf, and mittens when I heard a loud crashing sound come from the backyard. I went out to see what it was and found the corn crib leaning precariously on three legs. The ice had built up on the roof of the old structure and caused it to cave in on one corner. We had planned to take it down in the spring anyway, so I didn't worry about it.

As I turned to go back to the house, turn out the lights, and head for the road, I heard a horn beeping out front. I ran through the house, turned off lights, and dashed out the front door only to see the school bus driving on down the road. This was a disaster! I'd waited for this day all year.

At the school, everyone was preparing for their class Christmas Parties. My mom had her second-grade room all decorated with snowflakes and tinsel and my room had homemade Christmas cards lining the doors and tables set up for tons of "food!". The principal was playing Christmas music on the loudspeaker and many of the parents were there to hand out small gifts. This was going to be the greatest school day in history. How could I have messed up and missed the bus? What to do.......

At about 9:00 that morning, there was an announcement on the loudspeaker from the principal, Mr. Call. "Would the owner of the tractor parked in the teacher's parking lot please come to my office?" I paused, tried to think of a story, and went to the office. My mom was already there and didn't look very festive. "O.K., start talking. How did our tractor get into that parking lot?"

I stammered and stuttered and did my best to explain what had happened. I didn't want to miss the party and it was just there. Much to my surprise, they broke into laughter and sent me back to my classroom without any punishment. Dad came by with Dick that night and Dad followed Dick home with the car. Sometimes you have to be a little creative to reach your goals. I was lucky I didn't get hurt and I had such wonderful, understanding parents.

Luke 2:13-14   "And suddenly there was with the angel a multitude of the heavenly host praising God and saying, Glory to God in the highest, and on earth peace, good will toward men."

A quote seen on the wall of a church in Rural Retreat, VA: "The will of god will never take you

where the Grace of God will not protect you."

EYE FOR AN EYE

Adjacent to our farm and the Metro-park was a piece of property owned by an organization called The Exchange Club. There were approximately 10 acres with a large cabin situated on it that was used by civic organizations including The Boys Club, Boy Scouts, and Big Brothers. The long gravel drive from the main road led to the cabin that had a bunk house area, a spacious central room with a fireplace, and a huge stuffed black bear occupying one corner. The kitchen had a large wood-burning stove for cooking and behind the cabin were outhouses for boys and girls, along with the baseball diamond and outside cooking area. Every winter our scout troop would spend at least one weekend there to work on advancements and merit badges.

It was January of 1953 and we had just settled in for a fun weekend of both work and play. One of the boys was in the bunk room with some of his friends and was showing off his knife-throwing skills by hurling his hunting knife at a wall near the entry door. This was definitely not acceptable and was causing damage to the wall. Being the Senior Patrol Leader, I was informed about this and had to go put a stop to the infraction.

As I entered the room, unseen by the boys, the knife was thrown yet again and as it glanced off the wall and headed for my face there was no time to react. That big hunting knife struck me firmly across the right eye, causing a cut that unfortunately included the white part of my eye, ending the knife-throwing, but I had to be taken immediately to Medina Hospital where I was treated and released with a neat black patch to wear for a couple weeks.

The eye healed rather quickly, as did the cut on my face, but something was seriously wrong. Prior to the incident, I was a fluent reader and read everything I could get my hands on. Now, for some odd reason, I could only read one word at a time and after a short period, the words would start to scramble on the page.

Mom and Dad made an appointment with an eye specialist in Cleveland and he did several tests to determine the cause of the problem. Apparently, when the knife cut my eye, it damaged the nerve leading to the brain that feeds it information. This caused a delayed reaction and I could only see whatever I focused on. I had such a love for sports, but unfortunately, the problem was also apparent when I was playing baseball, especially when I played infield or catcher. I couldn't react fast enough to catch the ball and usually ended up getting hit, which made me feel like such a klutz. On the other hand, playing the outfield, I had time to focus on the ball and didn't have a problem.

The doctor said that there was nothing he could do but let time repair the problem, but over the years, it's never changed, so I've learned to live with it. Just like people who lose limbs, or have other disabilities, you learn to adjust and accept the challenge you've been given. They said I could never make it through college with this limitation, so I did. They said I could never be a writer, this is my second book. I haven't read a book from cover to cover in years, but I can still get the job done. The experience has given me tremendous respect for people with disabilities. I've learned that you don't do what your body tells you, you do what your heart tells you.

"Can't" is just a word, four letters by the way, and you don't have to accept it if your heart says you can. God gives us the strength to do amazing things in our lives and we just need to listen to Him. Whether you have a physical or mental disability; you can have a wonderful life if you choose, in your heart, to accept that disability and move on not wallow in pity. God will always be there to guide you and you will never be alone.

Psalms 23:1-6   "The Lord is my shepherd; I shall not want. He maketh me lie down in green pastures: he leadeth me beside the still waters. He restoreth my soul: he leadeth me in the paths of righteousness for his name's sake. Yea, though I walk through the valley of the shadow of death, I will fear no evil: for thou art with me; thy rod and thy staff they comfort me. Thou preparest a table before me in the presence of mine enemies: thou anointest my head with oil; my cup runneth over. Surely goodness and mercy shall follow me all the days of my life: and I will dwell in the house of the Lord forever."

CHRISTMAS

C hristmas on the farm was always a special time of year, and our very first Christmas was the foundation for all the Christmases to come. Each Christmas Eve we would go, as a family, to the back of the property, cut down a small pine tree, and bring it home to be placed in a stand in the living room. That evening we would all help decorate the tree and sing Christmas carols, Mom would read "The Night Before Christmas" and the special verses from the Bible about the birth of Jesus. Before we went to bed, we would set out cookies and milk for Santa, then Mom and Dad would tuck each of us in bed with a kiss goodnight, and a reminder that Santa didn't come until we were fast asleep.

Back in November, Dad installed a gas furnace in the basement and had taken out the old wood-burning stove in the living room that was used to heat the whole house. The old stove pipe had gone up through the ceiling and our bedroom so there was a hole about a foot in diameter left in our floor upstairs.

Christmas morning, I would wake to the sound of Mom's old Victrola playing Christmas songs and the smell of hot chocolate wafting up through that hole in the floor. That's where I would wake up, since that's where I fell to sleep: on the floor, with my pillow and feather tick, in my bathrobe and slippers, watching for Santa. I never did actually see him, since he always came after I fell asleep, but I knew he had stopped by because the cookies were eaten and the milk was gone and, also because I always got the special gift I had asked for in my letter to him. One year I asked for green plastic soldiers and there they were. Another year he brought the big, black Schwinn bike that I had longed for.

The year I turned nine, Dick came home from school one day in a really grumpy mood. I was sitting with pen and paper trying to decide what to ask Santa for when he blurted out, "There is no Santa!" That comment start a yelling match that brought Mom into the room. She calmly called Sue into the room and sat all three of us down and straightened the whole thing out. I'll never forget her speech:

"When you were good, Santa always brought you what you asked for. He always thanked you for the milk and cookies. He always left extra goodies in your stockings. And this is the most important thing to remember. "When you stop believing in him, he doesn't come anymore."

To this day, all of us try to relive that Family Christmas Tradition. And.......... Please don't tell me there is no Santa!

No verses here. Just a suggestion that YOU try to create YOUR OWN family tradition and maintain it through the generations; but don't forget that the real celebration is The Birth of Baby Jesus

Football Season

Football season has arrived. The cold weather, the snow and slush, the falling leaves, and tryouts for the team. It was my Freshman Year. Highland High had four years of high school and because it was so small, we had only about 40 guys trying out. My brother was a Senior and the big star fullback, so I got a ride to and from practice each afternoon. Practice was behind the school on cold slushy grass. Because I was 6 feet 3 inches tall and about 160 pounds soaking wet, the coach thought I might make a good offencive end. Every practice I might get one or two passes thrown in my direction. Usually out of reach. I think that the only reason I was even on the team was because the coach needed bodies to look like the team was bigger than it really was.

I remember one game in particular against Brunswick that is still etched in my mine. It was a night game under the lights. The field was covered with wet snow. They had to shoval the snow off the yard lines to find the first down markers. My position on the team was secure. I had three jobs that night. I was to play END, GUARD, and TACKLE. My job was to sit on the end of the bench, guard the water bucket, and tackle anyone who tried to steal it. I also was to be the first one off the bench to give my parka to the quarterback then there was a timeout. We won the game that night, 10 to 7. and rapped up the season 2 and 8, and I'm proud to say that noone got their hands on our water bucket.

Although I wasn't the big star, like my brother, I did get to wear my jursey around the school on the day of each game. Noone made fun of me because after football, I played basketball as the only Freshman on the Varsity Squad. I played first string Center because I was still the tallest kid in the school.

EPILOGUE

EPILOGUE

As I review the chapters of this book I reflect on the purpose of it all and the two main reasons for writing it.

One is to honor my wonderful, caring parents for the amazing life they created for my siblings and me. As I mentioned at the beginning of this book, "Childhood is the foundation of our lives". The three major aspects of parenting they taught me are; Love of family, Respect for each other, and Love of God. Now, today, in 2023 as I sit here writing this review, listening to Josh Groban in the background singing the very appropriate lyrics, "You raise me up to stand on mountains; You raise me up to more than I can be", I know this is what my parents did. I can only pray that you will have a chance to experience the same or, that you will raise your children with the similar guidelines and ideals that my parents gave to me. May the preceding stories give you some insight as to how they accomplished this feat with love, respect, guidance, understanding, direction, and a good ear which are all necessary in the raising of your children. Those childhood years seemed like a never-ending fantasy, and in most cases were, but there were difficult times too. We were taught to remember and treasure the good times and learn from both the good and the bad. I am always reminding my friends and acquaintances who have small children to enjoy every minute they can with their children because TOMORROW they're gone and off to be adults. The more good memories you can create with your children, the better person they will become, and that love and respect will be passed on to their children.

You don't have to be wealthy to give your children a good life. God knows, we weren't well-heeled financially, but we were the richest people on earth because we had each other. God truly blessed me with two wonderful parents and a pretty cool brother and sister.

The second purpose of this book was to, in a subtle way, re-introduce you to the Bible and to show you that everything we face in life is addressed somewhere within God's word. Guidance and answers abound on every page if we would only take the time to sit and read; think of experiences or problems you have had or have now and read; the answers are all there. If we will only open our hearts and minds to His word, our lives will change for the better. Again, I'm not a preacher or a learned scholar of theology, but my experience tells me that without God in our lives, we can never really experience true happiness and contentment. As a parent, I believe it's our responsibility to teach these foundations to our children; to teach by example as my parents did. It worked for me and it can work for you.

I truly hope you enjoyed the many stories of my childhood on my way to becoming the adult I am today. They're all true to the best of my recollection and some may remind you of your own experiences. The 40s and 50s were a wonderful time to grow up, but time is irrelevant because growing up in today's world can be just as exciting if you and your family make it so.

WHERE ARE THEY NOW?

Emil M. Blazak: My Dad, my mentor, and best friend. Dad worked for Western Union Telegraph Company for 50 years and then retired. In 2004, God called him home at the age of 95. I believe he still watches over me today and keeps me on the right track. In my eyes, he will always be a shining example for all fathers to follow.

Camilla J. Blazak: My Mom, guidance counselor, and my angel. Mom lived in her own home in Chattanooga, TN, and was a healthy 4 feet, 11-inch ball of energy. At 90 years old, she could still outwork and outplay any 50-year-old.

Dick Blazak: My brother, buddy, and successful building contractor. He married his high school sweetheart, Mary Ann, and went on to be very successful in Chattanooga where he recently retired and he and Mary Ann are working with the Red Cross Volunteer Program. They've been happily married for over 49 years and have two daughters and four grandchildren.

Susen J. Blazak (Batke): My sister, BFF (best friend forever), and Citizen of the Year for the Township of Hinckley, Ohio. Sue has been married for over 37 years to Ron and still lives in Hinckley in a home they designed and built themselves over 40 years ago. They have two daughters and one grandchild. Recently retired, they now spend their time traveling and working with their City.

Janet Bartel: My first girlfriend, classmate, and lifetime friend. Janet still lives in Hinckley and owns a beauty salon. We have kept in contact all these years and updated our lives at class reunions and via E-mail. A big "thank-you" goes to her for some of the information she reminded me of, since my mind is starting to fail.

The Famous Buzzards of Hinckley: Every March the Township has a National Buzzard Day to celebrate the coming of spring. People from all over the country come to watch these ugly birds land in the same tree, the same day, every year. (That tree, by the way, is right next to the old farm.) Check it out next March and enjoy a pancake breakfast, story telling, local music and a fun time. If you've never seen a real buzzard before, you haven't really seen it all.

The Perfect Love Story

This is a story about my two loving parents, Cam and Emil Blazak. You've read about the wonderful years of my childhood on the farm in Hinckley, Ohio. They gave us a life that most kids could only dream of. Now I'll jump ahead many years. They're lives together never changed. As a matter of fact, over time, it got even better. Their ages were seven years apart, but they were always a team.

In their 80's they moved to Chattanooga, TN and bought a little house near my brother. I was living in Atlanta about an hour and a half away. My Dad's favorite magazine was The National Geographic and he had saved about 50 copies, reading them over and over. Every once in a while he would see something that spiked his curiosity and he would react in the most alarming way. One time he was reading an artical about Egypt and he said to Cam "Honey! I've never ridden a camel. Let's go to Egypt and you can see the Pyramids and I can ride a camel." With that he picked up the phone and called a local travel agent and booked a round trip for two to Cairo.

On another ocassion he was reading about the Blarny Stone in Ireland and two weeks later he was on his back, kissing that dirty old stone while Cam looked on. Where ever they traveled, they were together. He wore the same outfit, his favorite string tie and a bright red sport jacket and they traveled hand in hand, thinking about their next trip together.

Several years later, my dad wanted to go back to Hinckley and see the old farm that we all loved and relive some of the wonderful memories. He was 95 now and had reluctantly given up his car keys a few years eariler. That was a challange for Dick and I because he had hidden about 5 sets of keys and every time we got his keys we would see him pulling out of the driveway on a trip to the store or to church. On his way home he'd pick off a couple mail boxes. Finally we wised up and took off the dirtributer cap and hid it.

I agreed to drive them up to Ohio and we stayed with my sister who has still living in Hinckley near the farm. What he didn't know was that the Hinckley Reservation that surounded the farm had bought the 50 acre farm and torn down the house and all the buildings. Everything had gone back to nature and the only way you could find the property was to find the three huge maple trees that still stood in front of where the house once stood.

Dad was heartbroken, but he decided that he wanted to hike back to the old campsite where he had spent so much quality time teaching scouting to hundreds of young boys over the years. Sue and Mom waited in the car and I went to get Dad and walk with him to the back of the property. I could still remember every hill and valley, every black berry patch, and what was now, the dirt trail about a mile to the campsite. But what I couldn't find was DAD. I called and called but no answer. I ran back to the car and told the girls what had happened. Sue called her husband Ron who was a Park Policeman and he called in his crew and the search was on.

I looked around for Mom and now she was missing. Sue and I called and called with no luck. I told her to wait at the car for Ron and his crew to arrive. It was getting dark and I had a hunch they were headed for the campsite, so I headed that way. The route to the campsite was etched in my mind and I knew I could find my way, even in the dark. It was a clear night and there was a three-quarter moon to light the way. It was like God had a flashlight and He was leading the way. When I reached the campsite I saw, to my surprise, a lighted area on the ground. It was like the star shining down on baby Jesus in Bethleham.

There, in the center of what used to be the campground, were Mom and Dad. Mom was sitting on the ground crying. Curled in her arms was Dad. He had gone home to GOD. I rushed over and held them both. Then something strange happened. I reached in my pocket and there was a book of matches there. I didn't remember ever having them in my pocket. I scrambled around and easily found dead branches to build a fire. Just six feet from us was the flag pole that was used to proudly hold our American Flag so many years ago. That fire light was seen by the searchers and help soon arrived. Mom stayed with Sue for a couple weeks and Dad was shipped back to Chattanooga.

Another strange thing that happened after that fateful day at the farm. As I drove home to Atlanta, everytime I looked up from the road, a single Buzzard was circling over head. I had this strange feeling that it was my dad, watching over me. This continued for seven years until my mom went to God on the same day and age as my dad. Then, to my amazement, TWO buzzards now fly overhead everytime I travel. God does work in mysterious ways. He makes sure that we are never alone. The only time those two guys arn't up there is when I'm driving to a Casino. He knows. Remember,

ONLY GOD CAN MAKE A BUZZARD!